OUR AFRICAN WINTER

"BILLIE"   A. C. D.   J. C. D.   DENIS   ASHTON JONSON   MALCOLM

DRAMATIS PERSONÆ

OUR AFRICAN WINTER

ARTHUR CONAN DOYLE

Duckworth

This edition published in 2001 by
Gerald Duckworth & Co. Ltd.
61 Frith Street, London W1D 3JL
Tel: 020 7434 4242
Fax: 020 7434 4420
Email: enquiries@duckworth-publishers.co.uk
www.ducknet.co.uk

First published in 1929 by
John Murray

A catalogue record for this book is available
from the British Library

ISBN 0 7156 3084 9

Typeset by Derek Doyle & Associates, Liverpool
Printed in Great Britain by
Bookcraft (Bath) Ltd, Midsomer Norton, Avon

PREFACE

This little book contains some impressions formed in South Africa, in Rhodesia, and in Kenya. They cover a good many political and economic points in addition to the particular question which was the object of our journey. It is the fashion to smile at the opinions of the passing traveller, and to label him as a globe-trotter, but when one has trotted as far over the globe as I have done one has a standard of comparison without which an opinion is worthless. It is to be remembered also that the man on the spot is influenced by all sorts of personal considerations, while the traveller is an impartial observer. At the same time his knowledge is admittedly superficial. He can but try to be honest in forming an opinion and fearless in expressing it.

ARTHUR CONAN DOYLE.

June, 1929.

CONTENTS

PAGE

CHAPTER I   11
The Start – Trouble in the Bay – British and Boers –
Madeira – The Death of de la Rey – Spiritualism and the
Christ – Lectures on the Ship – Some Dutch Friends –
End of the Voyage.

CHAPTER II   33
Reception at Cape Town – Nature's Mystery – A
Broadcast – The Dutch School – The Native Question –
Taking up a Farm – University Dinner – A Heresy Hunt
– Table Mountain – Bushman Paintings – First Lecture –
A Successful Séance – Strange Musical Mediumship – My
Wife's Protest – Meeting at Town Hall – Reincarnation.

CHAPTER III   57
Port Elizabeth – A Liberal Rabbi – "The Garden of
Death" – The Strange Canoe – Port Elizabeth –
Reminiscences of 1900 – Political Misunderstanding –
The Bywoner – Sanna's Post – I Meet Several Friends –
Maritzburg – The Voortrekkers – A Spirit Dog.

CHAPTER IV   81
Durban – The Valley of a Thousand Hills – Abduhl Latif,
an Evidential Case – A Durban Séance – Dick King –
The Protection of Natives – Denis makes his Debut –
The Zulu Seer – Glorious Bathing – The East Indian
Problem.

CHAPTER V   101
The Eastern Transvaal – South African Problems – The
Native Strike – The Mean White – The Learned and the
Humble – The Rustenburg Spirit Photograph – The
Kruger Statue – Pretoria – Professor Kovaloff – A
Warning to Investors.

CHAPTER VI   117
South African Art – The Coming of the Fairies – Teetotal
Revelry – General Tanner – Louis Botha's Letters – The
Flag – The Robinson Mine – The Slums – The Native
Bazaar – Bishop Karney – Our Sunday Service – The
Premier Diamond Mine – The Future of Johannesburg.

CHAPTER VII   139
Bechuanaland – The Khami Ruins – The Matoppo
Hills – A Psychic Interlude – The Victoria Falls – The
Rain Forest – *Livingstone's Journal* – A Rhodesian
Farm – Bitter Political Feeling – General Prospects of
Rhodesia.

CHAPTER VIII   163

Chances in Rhodesia – Salisbury – A Remarkable House – Jan Ridd – The Umtali Murder – A Transvaal Case – Sally of Rhodesia – The Missions – A Personal Note – Farewell to Rhodesia.

CHAPTER IX   185

A Giant's Playground – The Pungwe Marshes – Beira – A Cyclone – A Great Ray – Chicoa Silver Mines – The Gospel of St. John – Mandated Territory – Mombasa.

CHAPTER X   199

A Sporting Colony – The Railway Zoo – The Asiatic Question – Miss Mayo's Book – A Day's Hunting – Drinking Habits – Tarlton's Farm – Native Question – Economics – The American Zola – A Lost Farm – The Man-eater – Psychic Experiences – John Boyes.

CHAPTER XI   227

We start for the Great Lake – The Rift Valley – A Dangerous Road – The Gulf of Kavirondo – *Darkened Rooms* – Tanganyika – The Mwanza Jail – The Bishops – Native Football – The Source of the Nile – A Cloud.

CHAPTER XII   243

The People of Nairobi – Strange Animals – A Lecture Incident – Mombasa – The Famous Siege – An Earth-bound Animal – Salt Water once more.

CHAPTER XIII   253
A Lonely Ocean – Solomon's Tanks – *The Nation's Key-men* – A Great City of the Future – A Dead Town – A Crowded Day – The Great Pyramid – Malta – Home Again.

APPENDIX   271

CHAPTER 1

The Start – Trouble in the Bay – British and Boers – Madeira – The Death of de la Rey – Spiritualism and the Christ – Lectures on the Ship – Some Dutch Friends – End of the Voyage.

It is a foul morning, and yet in two hours we have to be aboard the *Windsor Castle* which awaits us at Southampton. Our country cottage at Bignell Wood is only seven miles from the port and the motor is waiting at the door. My heart sinks as I sit at my desk in the window of my room and look through the blurred panes at the lashing rain and see the yellow leaves streaming across the lawn, while the wind howls through the half-bare branches of the great oaks and beeches which hem us in. It must be blowing a full gale in the Channel. Personally as an old whalesman I am not concerned with the weather. But it is a rude start for those who are – especially for my wife, who is sensitive to the sea. It is one of the many sacrifices which she makes for our cause, that she leaves a home which she loves to embark upon voyages which do not attract her. All that I can do to mitigate the ordeal is to bring the three youngsters along, so that she may not be separated from them.

This is the fourth of the long journeys which we have all five made upon the same errand – the errand of spreading the discussion of certain facts which we both think it is essential for the world to know. In 1920-1 we did Australia and New Zealand. Then we had two journeys in '22 and '23 which carried us all over America and Canada, and now it is South Africa. This is surely the last.

It is not merely upon my psychic quest that I go. My health has been somewhat run down and I would escape the English winter. Then too I wish to show my family some of the places which were familiar to me in the days of the Boer War, and to write some small account of the country which should touch upon economic and political conditions as well as upon our psychic adventures. The latter, so far as I am committed at present, consist only of two lectures at Cape Town, but I shall be surprised if they stop there. I thought it wise not to promise too much.

And now they are calling me from the front and I see them clustering round the motor. Those who have been good enough to take an interest in my first book of travel, *The Wanderings of a Spiritualist* would hardly recognize us now. Denis and Malcolm have grown into two splendid young giants, six feet and broad in proportion.

The child whom we still call Billy is budding into womanhood. They are all old enough to be of help now in their several ways. They will do some of my excessive secretarial work, but my good friends Mr. and Mrs. Ashton Jonson are waiting at Cape Town and will give me their very capable assistance – which is the more valuable as they are both well versed in psychic matters. So now we are off with every prospect of a few days of discomfort before we reach the warmer, calmer waters across the bay.

The days of discomfort came all right and the width of the Bay of Biscay separates this paragraph from the last one. We have gone through it amid a terrible gale and a mighty roll which are said by the old sailors to have been unprecedented. Ten degrees is supposed to be a pretty fair roll, but at our best effort we did thirty, which approaches the margin of safety. It certainly passed the margin of personal stability, for there have been many accidents and several passengers have been badly cut or bruised. Denis had three bad falls and Malcolm one, but the ladies wisely kept their cabins. Personally I served my apprenticeships in small vessels, and the worst which the weather can do to an 18,000-ton liner seems a small thing when one has lived in the Arctic in a 250-ton barque. However it was, even from my point of view, quite bad enough.

It was magnificent, however. I stood at the weather rail and I saw those wonderful Atlantic combers racing towards us, dark slate with veins of silver, and a tossing, creaming crest above. It is hard to measure them with the eyes, but I should think from trough to summit some 30 or 40 feet might be a fair estimate, and sometimes two coming from different angles would well up together and make a pyramid of swirling, foaming, frantic water far higher than our highest deck. The wind and the spray struck you in the face and took your breath away. Our little flat in Victoria Street seemed a long way off – something in another world.

There was a comic side to it. Denis helped several old gentlemen who were rolling about on the floor of the lounge. One of them had his arms and legs wrapped round one of the pillars, and was found in the same position when Denis returned some time later, his eyes fixed with a glassy stare upon the rollers outside. Well, we are out of it now, and should not have any more trouble before we reach Madeira. And yet as I write these lines I recall that we are steaming over the scene of Trafalgar, that the battle was fought, if I remember right, late in October, and that it was followed by such a storm that the prizes were nearly all sunk. So we may not be out of danger yet, and the sky is not reassuring.

I had a long talk to-day with a British South African of some standing and experience. I must check it up by a similar talk with a Dutchman. The Englishman's view is that all is not well in South Africa, and that he and his kind are glad that Rhodesia, to say nothing of Kenya and the North, have not come into the Union. Natal, he says, would gladly get out of it. This was a sad hearing to me, who had hoped that the Dominion was contented and prosperous. As to the flag, it seems to me natural enough that a land which has been settled and developed in the first instance by the heroism and industry of Dutchmen should wish to have some sign of its own which should differentiate it from places like New Zealand or Australia, which are all British. Why should they not have their own distinctive sign so long as they are within the Empire? My friend's contention, however, was that a strong party did not desire to remain in the Empire, but would found a republic, contrary to the Peace of Vereeniging. If such a course were pursued, it would indeed be terrible, since it would certainly lead to civil war. Fortunately, however, there are many splendid Dutchmen of the Smuts type who have respect for the promise given, and would never side with their rebellious countrymen, should such an issue ever be raised. We can never forget how nobly a number of the Boers rallied to the flag in the Great War, or how great a fiasco was the rising of De Wet and de la Rey.

Still, the fact remains that there seems to be a regrettable amount of British dissatisfaction which arises from numerous pinpricks. "It is in the country districts that we feel it," said my informant. "The ignorant bywoner predominate there, and every case is brought before a Dutch magistrate who has to please his neighbours, and will not give the Englishman a dog's chance." This may be exaggeration, and perhaps fuller knowledge will put a different colour upon it. I hope so.

Here we are at Madeira, safe and sound, and the first stage of our journey is done. It was good to put our feet on solid ground after that infernal experience in the Bay. The officers have assured me since that they never had such a doing before and hope never to have it again. Hard-boiled as I am as a traveller, I am heartily of the same way of thinking.

The lads went off at Funchal seeking adventures as lads will, while "Billy", my daughter, with my wife and self, went by cog-wheel up to the mountain to the spot, some 3,000 feet up, whence one of the views of the world can be obtained. In my experience I can only compare it with the Tibidabo view behind Barcelona, and the view from the mountain across the bay from San Francisco. It was cloudy and raining, but between the drifting wreaths, we got wonderful framed pictures of the gulfs which lay on each side, and of the distant Bay of Funchal, with our great steamer as a little toy boat on the edge of the water. We descended in toboggans, clattering over the ridged cobblestones, an adventure which is amusing at first but becomes tiring before you have finished 4 miles of it. What amused us most was the pathetic optimism with which the Madeirans imagined that they were going to sell us things. As we flew past on a toboggan a mahogany-faced old lady stood by the track with an ingratiating smile, holding out a tablecloth which she clearly expected us to buy in transit. To the last moment they pestered us, and we looked back astern expecting to see them swimming in our wake with garden chairs, parrots in cages, and other inconceivable truck. Their incessant importunity takes something from the pleasure of the island.

And yet it is a sweet little place – entirely volcanic and possibly a relic of the great Atlantean disaster. Anyhow, it lies just where the priests of Hieropolis told Solon that the old continent used to be. We carried away a pleasant memory of the subtropical vegetation, the sugar-cane, banana, vine and cactus, gradually changing to fir and oak as one ascended. Purple bugainvillia covered the walls. Only a sailor can really appreciate flowers.

In connection with the Atlantis theory there was one point which seemed to me to be of importance. At one side of the island is a sheer cliff which is said to be the highest seacliff in the world, a perpendicular drop of 2,000 feet, which is continued for several thousand more feet under water. That offers a most curious problem. Much depends upon whether the face of the cliff is true rock or Plutonic. But, in any case, how could one possibly explain such a structure by erosion or any other geological supposition? Suppose, however, that it was really a broken-off corner of old Atlantis, and that as the continent sank this rock split and the old edge of the country remained at its proper level while the rest went under the waves, then we have a clear reason for that monstrous cleavage. In that case Madeira is not an island which rose volcanically from below, but it is the corner of a vanished continent, still buried in the debris which was shot out at that fearful convulsion. Putting theory to one side, there remains at least the undeniable fact that here in the very place where ancient legend has placed Atlantis we have clear evidence of tremendous volcanic action – and that this Cabro Girao, as it is called, does present the appearance of a titanic fracture.

Now we are at sea once more, passing the Canary Islands. I had an interesting conversation with a South African, who was in a position to know, in which he told me the amazing particulars of the death of the Boer leader, General de la Rey. It is, as it seems to me, beyond the range of coincidence, and to have been a direct intervention of Providence to prevent the disruption of the British Empire. This is the story, and it is a credulous mind which can suppose that nothing but Chance was at work.

Upon the outbreak of war in 1914 Botha and Smuts, with other Boer leaders, were splendidly loyal. Beyers, however, who was the actual head of the army, was a traitor, and endeavoured to drag with him the venerable and honoured leader de la Rey, who was a very old man but a great force among his countrymen. Beyers drove from a review of Union troops in Pretoria in order to attend a great gathering of armed Boers at Potchefstroom, where he intended to proclaim a republic. He was in a grey Talbot car, accompanied by de la Rey, and their route lay through Johannesburg.

It happened that there had been a series of bank robberies in Johannesburg by a man named Foster, and it was known that this desperado had a grey Talbot car. Therefore pickets of police had been stationed round the town, with orders to stop any car of that description.

As Beyers entered the town he saw these armed pickets, which did not challenge him, as he was coming in and not out. His guilty conscience took alarm, however, and he ordered his chauffeur to drive hard and not stop if challenged. He was naturally challenged as he left the town, and as the chauffeur obeyed his orders and disregarded the challenge, the men fired at the ground, hoping to burst the tyres. The bullets ricochetted off the hard road and killed de la Rey, who was seated behind.

There was the end of Beyers' plot, but Fate had not yet worked out its complete plan. Had matters ended there it would certainly have been spread through Africa that de la Rey had been assassinated in order to prevent a rising. How could the high directing forces prevent such a conclusion, which might have caused civil war just as surely as the declaration of a republic would have done? No human ingenuity could have invented a method so direct and yet so ingenious as that which actually occurred.

There was a Dr. Grace in Johannesburg, an Englishman, who also drove a grey Talbot car. What romancer would have dared to put three of them on the road at the crisis of his story! This doctor was summoned to an accident outside Johannesburg that day, and he ordered his chauffeur to drive at top speed. The man disregarded the signals of the police, they fired as before, and Dr. Grace was killed in exactly the same way as de la Rey. Even the most suspicious Boer was bound to admit that as an Englishman had met the same fate as the Dutchman, it was clearly not a plot of the British party. A great issue – a very great issue – was at stake, and I do not know where in history one can see more direct evidence of intelligent forces working to a preconceived end.

As to Beyers he was hunted down, though not before he had dragged De Wet into his plot. It is a matter of history how splendidly many of the Boers rallied to the Empire, and two of de la Rey's sons were among the volunteers.

Apropos of such apparent interpositions of Providence, a passage which I read to-day in Flammarion's *La Mort et son mystère* seems as if it were written to meet such a case. He says: "Ne remarquons nous pas de temps en temps dans les evénements humains certaines occurrences semblant indiquer l'existence d'une justice immanente? Est il intredit d'admettre l'action d'etres invisibles dirigeant les choses? La fourmi ne voit pas le pied qui l'ecrase. Les microbes regissent notre santé sans que nous les voyions."

On November 1st we passed close to Cape de Verde and natives in canoes could be seen from the deck. I don't know if there is still a large white staff at the telegraph station there, but I remember that in the Boer War time they were numerous enough to make a very fair cricket Eleven which played each transport as it halted there. Knowing the conditions and playing on matting they were, I believe, undefeated until our ship came along and beat them. I had a good day both with bat and ball – *Eheu fugaces.*

People imagine that a long voyage must be restful and peaceful, but really it may become more strenuous than ordinary life. For example, we have a French lesson morning and evening under the tuition of a French acrobat from the second class. There is an interminable list of competitions of various kinds for the youngsters. There is a daily swim for every one in the big salt-water bath. There are concerts and dances every evening. I have been asked to lecture upon psychic subjects on Sunday. Add to this the constant companionship, the writing of letters, and the use of a good library, and no one should find time hang heavy. But the heat is already rather trying as we approach the Equator.

We were hardly over the line, however, before we ran into an excellent head wind which has made the voyage a very comfortable one. We have after our many wanderings become connoisseurs of steamship lines. The general standard of comfort and efficiency is very high, but I should certainly put this vessel, the *Windsor Castle*, under her genial captain Sir Benjamin Chave, at the very top of our list. She may not have the luxury of the great Atlantic liners, but she has a homely, happy atmosphere which more than atones. Our voyage will ever be a pleasant memory, in spite of the one boisterous experience.

One benefit of such a voyage is that even amid the clatter of deck quoits and the everlasting gramophone one does get hours when one can steal away and be alone with one's thoughts and with nature. The best time, I find, is just after sunset, when in the upper deck you can find some lonely corner and look out at a dark semicircle of ocean which shades away into great grey drifting clouds with peeps of melon- and salmon-tinted sky showing through the rifts. Even as a passenger in a crowded ship such a night is overpowering, but how would it be if one were in an open boat, alone, and with nothing in sight save that circle of water and that tremendous arch of heaven? One would surely, feel more face to face with God than in any position which earth could give.

At such times I naturally think much of my own religious position and question my own soul as to its essential soundness. Of that I can have no possible doubt – I have tested it too often and too thoroughly. Far from weakening it grows upon me, and I see more clearly that this revelation is the most important which mankind has ever had and that we who are spreading it are doing the most vital work that is done in the world to-day. But is it entirely on the right lines? On that I have my doubts. I feel a sympathy for those who desire that the movement should be kept quite unconnected with any special creed. It is a broad, noble ideal. But it is not practical and it blocks the way and hinders our advance. If all religions are to be drawn together by this new knowledge there should be two stages, not one, in the process. The first stage should be that each great religion should separately within its own ranks learn and admit the new revelation. Then the second stage should be that all religions, finding that they have this definite knowledge in common, should draw closer to each other. But the first stage is essential, and that is what our leaders have not seen. In a Christian civilization it is necessary that the personality and ethics of the Christ should be proclaimed in connection with our psychic knowledge, and that the two should be joined together. We cannot object to the Jew adding it to his Mosaic teaching, or the Mohammedan to the teaching of the prophet, but in every case the old should not be abandoned too readily in order to substitute the new. I do not of course in our own case advocate dogma or fixed ritual. Theology has always been the enemy of real religion. But I do wish to see on the part of the Spiritualists of Christian countries some broad public acknowledgment of the work of that great teacher who twenty centuries ago said words and did deeds which even now have not been fully understood, but which certainly have had a wonderful influence upon the world. A European Spiritualist should in a broad sense be a Christian, and we shall never sweep through the nations until this is understood.

I have said that I think the message of Jesus has been misunderstood. I believe that it was in truth the same that we are giving to-day – namely, that man retains his personality after death in a world not unlike this one, and that his condition there depends upon his actions. A great deal of the subsequent dogma and ritual seem to have been added centuries later, and they are often derived from and are a compromise with Paganism. We have to remember that up to Christ's time the Jews had no clear idea of any after life. In the whole of the Old Testament there is hardly any allusion to it. Then the Christ came with His perfectly definite and material statements, very like our own, in which He talks of people sitting at His right hand, of many mansions, of drinking the juice of the grape, with other allusions which showed that life carried on. The idea is so familar to us that we can hardly imagine how exciting it was to the first who heard and accepted it. Hence their repeated ejaculations that the grave had lost its victory and death had lost its sting. When He actually reappeared in person and was seen by many then the cup of their joy was filled, since it was now clear that His teaching about survival was true. Paul said that unless the resurrection was true then the bottom dropped out of Christianity, so that he evidently regarded the proof of continued life to be the crucial point. It was the additional strength given to them by this proof which turned the apostles from being the cowards of Gethsemane to the heroes and martyrs of the early Church.

Well, I must get back to mundane things. We are now two days from our destination and everything is closing down. The family have not done badly on the voyage. My two big boys Malcolm and Denis have both been in the first-class tug-of-war team which pulled over all rivals. Denis is the champion at deck tennis. Billy was in the final of deck bowls and in the ladies' cricket Eleven: not so bad when one considers that there were in each case at least fifty competitors. In the big cricket match Billy took two wickets in two balls and was the only lady with an overhand delivery.

For my own part I have done some serious reading, including Drayton Thomas's *Life beyond Death, with Evidence*, which has an excellent preface by Lady Grey of Fallodon. This Wesleyan clergyman is, I think, destined to be a noted leader in our movement, for he has all the gifts – a pleasing personality, good platform delivery, a logical, clear-cut mind, and a remarkable power of exposition. I hope the day may come when he too will go round the world as I have done. His book is a very good one, hampered only by its high price, which is inevitable with books which find a difficulty in reaching the general public and appeal to a special class of readers. The day will come, and soon, when people will recognize that such literature is the most important and the most absorbing in the world. There will be no talk of limited editions then. I have read also Captain Campbell's book on his adventures in the Q boats – a wonderful man with the proper mixture of brain and courage which makes the hero of practical use. There are passages there – notably the account of the after gun on the *Dunraven* which should stand with the *Birkenhead* or with the sinking of the *Revenge* as British epics. I am not sure that the *Dunraven* does not stand supreme. There were six men concealed round the gun, and the ship, together with the magazine, was on fire beneath them. It was all-important to continue the pretence that the vessel was a harmless tramp, and so to tempt the submarine to rise. The plates grew hot beneath them, at any moment the magazine might explode, and yet they lay as still as mice. Finally the magazine *did* explode and they were all blown into the air. One was shot up to some spot near the captain, and he at once staggered forward and apologized for leaving his post without orders. Could discipline and bravery go further?

On the top of my reading and of keeping this discursive journal up to date, and of struggling, with a French conversation morning and evening, I have given lectures in each of the three classes upon my own psychic experiences and my deductions from them. My audiences have seemed to be deeply interested, and I hope I have given them some happiness and revised their notions of death. In each case I have called for written questions and have answered them on the spot. The questions have, as a rule, been very intelligent, and there was a pleasing absence of those references to texts which hamper all reasonable discussion. Some of the points raised have really been ingenious, though I think I have always been able to satisfy the questioner. One asked

– a third-class passenger too – "Why is it that in *Encephalilis lethargica* the spirit, if it exists, does not prevent the man from being buried alive, as often happens?" Another very good one is: "Why is it that savage races which have all practised spirit intercourse are in so low a state of development?" I have really answered that question in my previous writings where I have shown that independent ethical development must go with Spiritualism. A savage circle would attract savage spirits who would roughly be in the same state of development. I think that a good Spiritualist who could teach the truth of these matters would knock out the medicine man more quickly than the missionary could do.

I had a good chat this morning with a fine type of Boer, one Colonel Collins, who fought against us with his people, but afterwards fought for us in the Great War. He was strongly of the opinion that my English friend already quoted was misinformed and that there was no discrimination between races. The present Union will continue, according to him, and the Republican party are really negligible. He seems a very fine fellow and gained his D.S.O. in the British service. As he is a member of the legislative body he should have a fairly clear view of the situation. He admitted, however, that those Boers who fought for the British were unpopular with the more extreme Dutchmen, and were called "Khaki Boers" by them. There is, as it seems to me, a considerable analogy with the conflict of races in Canada, and no more chance of a secession.

Sir John Wessels, a famous judge in the High Court, gave me independently the same view that Colonel Collins had given. I remarked to him that the only desire in Britain was that the Dutch should have every possible constitutional right, and that the only thing which could and would lead to war would be the breaking of that golden circlet of Empire which is represented by the British Crown. I added that the latent feeling on that point was very deep and strong, and that this factor should be recognized before steps were taken which might bring it out. He said that there was no chance of a secession in the present generation. It was a fact, however, that the Dutch on the land were multiplying fast, and that there was little immigration save that of money-making Jews who, having made their fortunes, cleared out of the country, and were of no real use to the land which had provided their wealth. There was a certain British immigration and there were more on the land than of old, but they were too fond of combining tennis and other games with their farming, and did not take their work seriously, so that they were no match for Boer farmers who were used to the droughts and locusts and other peculiarities of the country. He did not think that there was any friction between the two races in the country, but there was a certain antagonism between the townsman, usually British, and the farmer, usually Dutch. I must say that the Dutch point of view seems to me to be a very moderate and reasonable one.

My day has been full of interesting and profitable conversations, for in the evening I had one with our commander Sir Benjamin Chave, a fine upstanding specimen of a British seaman. He told me of his adventures in the War, trooping to South-West Africa, trooping to Basra, and finally torpedoed in the mouth of the Channel. In a rough sea he launched six boats, two of which were never heard of more. Of the four others one made Liverpool, one made Corunna, and the captain himself was picked up and carried to New York. Half the men in the boats died of exhaustion. The merchant service bred heroes in those days. Incidentally the captain told me that our situation in the Bay, which I have treated rather lightly in my narrative, was really rather serious.

The barometer was at 28°, or under, which is the lowest I can ever remember in my sea rambles, save once when we were nearly blown out of the water in my whaling days. A woman passenger amused my wife by telling her that at the height of the gale a cadaverous steward poked his head into her cabin and said, "There is something radically wrong."

There should, I think, be some inquiry into the condition of the stewards aboard our big liners. It is not merely that their work is incessant, often fifteen hours a day, but it is that there is not enough provision made for their comfort. I have heard an old steward say that save in ports he has never had a single meal aboard the ship which was not taken standing. They are a fine lot of men and deserve more consideration. Their treatment varies, in different lines. The wages average about two pounds a week, with precarious tips in addition. This might pass if the conditions were ameliorated. Too many passengers seem to regard them as machines whose human wants may be disregarded.

Well, here we are at the last evening and every one is sitting among their trunks. Looking back, it cannot be said to have been a very pleasant voyage so far as the weather goes; but it has, as I have said, been a happy ship with a good captain and pleasant companions. To-morrow early we shall lie in Table Bay, ending one chapter of our lives and beginning another. It seems a long time since that morning with which my narrative begins, when the wet wind howled through Bignell Wood and I looked out of the streaming panes of my study windows and saw the autumn leaves of Hampshire fluttering across the lawn.

CHAPTER II

Reception at Cape Town – Nature's Mystery – A Broadcast –
The Dutch School – The Native Question – Taking up a Farm
– University Dinner – A Heresy Hunt – Table Mountain –
Bushman Paintings – First Lecture – A Successful Séance –
Strange Musical Mediumship – My Wife's Protest – Meeting
at Town Hall – Reincarnation.

We have now nearly finished our time in Cape Town, and my impressions are so numerous and so confused that unless I try at once to set them in order I shall never get them disentangled. Let me then take events as they came.

Early on Monday, November 12th, we found ourselves steaming slowly across the magnificent bay, now empty, but crowded when last I saw it with fifty transports. On the right, as we approached the quays, lay long new suburbs, rosy in the light of dawn, stretching out to Sea Point. Villas too, peeping out of woody slopes, were climbing up all the foothills, with the huge sombre bulk of Table Mountain towering behind them. It was clear to me that the town had considerably extended. Its population has indeed reached the respectable total of 127,000.

It was hardly six o'clock when we came alongside the quay, but already there was quite a group of people to meet us. Mr. and Mrs. Ashton Jonson, our faithful allies, were there, and so were a bunch of local Spiritualists, bearing flowers for my wife and for Billy. What with pressmen, photographers, a cinema fiend, custom-house officials and representatives of the African Theatres, Ltd., who are running my lectures, we had a hectic two hours. Presently, however, we broke away and found ourselves in the happy solitude of the fine Mount Nelson Hotel, which stands in a class by itself among South African establishments, and would take a high place if it were in England. Mr. Green, the manager, is assiduous in his care of his guests.

Certainly I know no hotel in England which offers such a panorama as is visible from the windows of our sitting-room. On the one side we look down upon the glorious but deadly bay, curving round in a huge semi-circle, with the low-lying leper island at the mouth, and the bare uplands upon the farther side. Beneath us lies the town – a huddle of red roofs and grey pinnacles. From the other window we look straight at the mighty mass of Table Mountain, one of the most monstrous blocks of isolated rock that the world can show. I am perpetually faced by the unsolved mystery of geology –

a science which will, I am convinced, be suddenly revolutionized by the advent of some great genius. Here are the alternate strata of sand and rubble in front of me on that huge rocky face, exactly as they lie in the quarry in front of my house at Crowborough, and exactly as the chalk and the flint alternate in the big chalk quarry at Wokingham or the coal and clay in a coal-seam. Is it not clear that there is a slow rhythmic rise and fall, a steady secular breathing of the old planet, which brings its surface now to the water's edge, and now above it?

On Tuesday night I was asked to broadcast a message from the Cape Town centre, which, covers a radius of a thousand miles or so. I thought it was a good opportunity to break ground and to define my own psychic position and the objects of my mission. I will transcribe what I said, as the reader may be glad to have a clearer view of the matter. I spoke thus:

"It is difficult in the few minutes at my disposal to give you a clear view of the psychic question. I hope to do it at greater length and with full illustration in my two lectures upon the 21st and the 26th. But there are a few words which I may say now which will help you to understand what is at issue.

"You may remember that last year Sir Arthur Keith, speaking with all the authority which belongs to a President of the British Association, said that in his opinion, and in the opinion of Science, death ends all.

There is no after life. This was corroborated by the great surgeon Sir W. Bland Sutton, and it was clear that his view met with a great deal of support. The effect produced upon my mind was that a considerable minority, if not the majority, of the British people, have come to hold this view. The statistics show that not more than 1 in 10 belong to any organized religious body.

"Now it is surely clear that if this view prevails it really knocks the bottom out of all Religion, as we understand Religion. If there is no after life, why should man strive to improve himself? It is a waste if all his efforts end in annihilation. I can conceive that earnest and noble men like Keith himself would continue to do duty for duty's sake; but I am sure that the mass of mankind would argue that if there is only one life, and death ends all, our wisest course is to get as much pleasure as we may.

The situation can only be met in one way. That one way is to *prove* that life exists after death – to prove it with scientific proof so as to meet Science upon its own ground. There is no use pleading Faith with those who have no faith. Now we Spiritualists are prepared to prove that we survive death. Our proofs are in my opinion absolutely final and certain. Nothing is evidence to those who will not examine the evidence; but those who have really examined it, including many of the best brains of the human race, have nearly all accepted it. If such men as Sir Oliver Lodge, Sir William Crookes or Professor Alfred Russell Wallace find it good enough, then it is mere folly to dismiss it without examination.

"Thus you see that we Spiritualists are defending what is the very heart and core of religion. We are proving the fundamental basis upon which all religion rests. That under these circumstances we should be opposed by the Materialists is natural enough. Our views are diametrically opposed. But that the clergy should oppose us is indeed a strange phenomenon. They must realize that the question at issue is not now between one sect and another sect, but the issue is between those who have some religion and those who have no religion. In opposing us they are really opposing their own best allies. Already however, I am glad to say, many of the more enlightened of the clergy are beginning to understand this, and I have observed a great change in England in the last few years. Recently I addressed an audience consisting entirely of clergy, and we found ourselves in complete accord.

"Our message is, of course, to all. We esteem all creeds and help all. The Jew, the Moslem, or the Buddhist has to die, even as we have, and our exact knowledge of what occurs at death and after death applies to him as well as to us. But, above all, it is a message of inexpressible consolation to the bereaved heart which we bring. All fear of death vanishes. The farther we probe into these mysteries the more convinced we become of the essential goodness and wisdom of the Creator, and that the future brings with it a promise of deep happiness, which is as much superior to our present condition as the sun at midday is to the sun at dawn.

"That is the message which we bring – and in 2,000 years no more important or more inspiring one has been delivered to the human race. I should be proud indeed if my visit to this wonderful country induced the inhabitants of it to look more closely into the matter, for nothing more important *could* possibly engage their attention."

This message was, I believe, well received, and lessened if it did not exclude those theological animosities which are so easily aroused.

We have run into beautiful weather – much the same as a fine English summer. For the information of possible visitors, especially those in search of health, be it stated that from September to March this is a land of sunshine and flowers – the latter more profuse than anywhere else. It is said that on Table Mountain alone there are more genera than in all England. There are at least two good golf courses, each of which I have already sampled; there is wonderful bathing, surf-riding and fishing, and there are very many beautiful drives. The tired man could not possibly do better than try the double voyage with this pleasant turning-point in which to rest.

The amenities of life also are surprisingly high. Thus I have been to-day to the Michaelis Gallery, where, housed in the appropriate setting of a Colonial Dutch house, one may see a small but very choice collection of pictures of the Dutch school. It is not, I confess, a school which has ever attracted me, for while one cannot but admit the technical perfection, the subjects are always of the earth earthy. The most perfect representation by Hondecoeter or Van Beyeren of a group of hens, or of a dead codfish and lobster, cannot move me more than such objects would actually do in life. I ask for imagination and spirituality, or the subject is not worth the trouble. In portraiture it is a different matter, and here we have wonderful reproductions of the picturesque burghers and their solid wives, even as they lived, with the extraordinary laced collars and cuffs which speak of a race of marvellous laundry women. For those who admire them – and I have no doubt I am in a minority – are fine specimens of Van Dyck, of Franz Hals, of Teniers, of Ruysdael, and others. The sea pieces are certainly magnificent.

There is another more modern collection of pictures, and there is an admirable Museum which is arranged most skilfully by a very competent curator, Mr. Lawrence Gill. Here one can see instructive models of the various native races, some of them actual moulds. It is curious how sharply these various types are divided from each other. In Europe there is an amalgam everywhere with only broad general averages of difference. Here in South Africa you have the little clever Bushman, now practically extinct, the larger Hottentot with hair like cloves stuck in a cake, and finally the magnificent man of the Bantu tribes, the Zulu or Matabele, one of the grandest physically of all human creatures. Each, in a pure specimen, is entirely distinct from the other.

The native question occupies a considerable place in the minds of thoughtful men in South Africa. There has been education and there has been Bolshevist teaching, and now there are dark swirls and eddies dimly visible down in the black depths. The whites in the country are under 2 million. The blacks are over 7 million. Then you have self-contained black countries such as Basutoland and the lands of the North. The present rate of increase is all against the whites. The danger is not immediate, but it is a very real one for the future. The only solution would seem to lie in greatly accelerated immigration.

At present this immigration, so far as the Briton is concerned, is limited to the man with capital who is ready to take up agriculture. Men of that sort are not numerous. In the last few years, however, there has been an association formed to help Britons to settle upon the land. There had been a previous one in 1820 which brought out 3,000 settlers from whom 70,000 South Africans are said to trace their origin. Again, about the same number have been brought out. They are required to find some capital of their own, but they are nursed along, and given opportunities of trying different forms of farming before they settle down. It is stated that up to now only 3 per cent of these immigrants have proved to be failures, whereas in similar schemes in Canada and Australia the failures have been 45 and 35 per cent respectively. So says Sir Charles Crewe, an authority upon the question.

As £2,000 was quoted as the capital needed to start a farm where virgin ground was given to the farmer, I was interested to find out how this sum would be expended. Mr. Flemming, the South African author, gives the following figures for his own 1,000-acre farm which he cut out of the bare veld. Ten miles of fencing (£500), 400 sheep (£550), twelve cows (£100), sixteen oxen (£240), instruments (£100). Then he has his water supply, pumps, house to build, and much more, so that it will be seen that £2,000 is really a minimum figure. But once established he is self-supporting at the worst, and at the best might become a well-to-do man in a few years.

A fine new University has just been opened here with residential quarters for 400 students which have already been allotted. It clearly meets a want and will be self-supporting. From a British point of view it is not entirely a blessing, as it will cut off from the home country those streams of fine young South Africans who adorn our Rugby football fields as well as our class-rooms. The University Club invited us all to dinner and we had a pleasant evening, save that I had to make a speech which appeared to amuse them very much, as it consisted of reminiscences of my own old days at Edinburgh, when Barrie and Stevenson were both contemporaries and poor old Henley was enduring his periodical martyrdom at the hospital. His lines, "Beneath the bludgeonings of Fate, my head is bloody but unbowed," were not poetic fancy but a literal statement of fact. My audience were interested to know that Stevenson was the secretary of a psychic society, even in those early days. In one of his first letters to me he addressed me as "Dear Fellow-Spookist."

Apart from this new University there is always, of course, the old-established University of Stellenbosch. This is, however, largely Dutch, and also largely theological. There is at present a tremendous hubbub there because one of the Dutch theologians, one Du Plessis, has been brave and honest enough to associate himself with some of the conclusions of the higher criticism. He has actually said that since the Pentateuch describes the death of Moses it was not all written by Moses, and that as the Psalms refer to the Babylonian Captivity, which occurred hundreds of years after David's death, he could not have been the sole author of them. He has also cast a doubt upon the immaculate conception, though this doubt would seem a small thing beside the positive statement of the Evangelist who traces the pedigree of Jesus through Joseph to David. The result of the controversy has not yet been decided, but Synods are sitting and there is every sign that the four-square backveld Boer will be placated by the sacrifice of the heretic. It is almost exactly the same situation as arose here in South Africa over Bishop Colenso some seventy years ago, so that the Dutch Church would seem to be just that amount of time behind the Anglican. These impossible backward people, who deny what is obvious, never seem to realize that it is not the Devil but their own folly which fills the world with unbelievers. By forcing what is incredible upon people they obscure what is credible and cause the rejection of all.

Denis and I have taken such golf as we could get, as it is necessary for me to keep physically fit in view of the work before me. The two main courses, Wynburg and Mowbray, are flat and monotonous, but surrounded by lovely scenery, and very well kept. Both the fairway and the greens are surprisingly good in a land where grass does not grow readily. At Wynburg we saw in the Pavilion a great skin of a rock python killed on the course – quite enough to put a nervous golfer off his putt. I had meant to climb Table Mountain with the boys, but it was borne in upon me that in my seventieth year with nearly 17 stone to carry, and a blazing sun above me, it was hardly fair to the African Theatre Co., Ltd., who have guaranteed my appearance at these lectures. The boys have come back with the report of nine hours' tramp, and of a glorious 100-mile view from the summit. Denis nearly got a snake – or the snake him – it seems to have been a fifty-fifty chance. Malcolm got a scorpion and many of the insects which his heart loves. They are making a funiculaire which will make things easier for elderly gentlemen.

I have been examining some of the Bushman paintings taken from the inside of caves and transported to the Museum here. They are extraordinarily interesting, but not necessarily old, as I am told that there are some which represent Europeans. The various animals are depicted with the utmost fidelity, but the human figures are slurred and conventionalized. Perhaps there was some taboo against depicting the human, as there is now among Mohammedans. But the really interesting point is that these paintings are so like the paintings done by primeval man in the caves of Spain that when they are placed alongside each other they are practically the same, save that the old craftsmen were the more artistic. There cannot be any doubt that the same race did both, though the whole length of Africa lies between. In addition to this the Bushmen's women have an extraordinary deformity of their hind-quarters which is also found in the drawings and sculptures in Spain. The clear deduction is that the whole of Africa was inhabited by the little yellow men, and then that the big black negroid people, coming from some flank, gradually pushed them down until now there are only a handful of the poor creatures lurking in the Kalahari Desert. The Boers shot them down like vermin, but I fear that our own dealings with Tasmanian and other natives do not allow us to sit in judgment. The fact is that such things, however terrible, are very hard to avoid when the savages begin to spear the cattle of the invaders.

By the way the Bushman stock – I am trying to avoid the scientific jargon – seem to have had the bow, that most ingenious of all the devices of primitive man, from very ancient prehistoric days. It appears in their early rock paintings, just as it appears in the early rock paintings in Arizona. It must, one would think, have been indispensable both in war and in the chase, giving the possessor an enormous advantage over those who had it not. And yet the Australian savages, inventors of the ingenious boomerang, seem never to have heard of the bow, and what is stranger still the Maoris, who were a very advanced race, and the most skilful navigators of any primitive people, knew nothing of the bow – even within historical times. The great negroid races did not use the bow, and I saw to-day a cave picture where the little brown men were cheekily driving off the cattle of the negroes, and covering the operation by a line of bowmen, who were holding off the blacks who pursued with shield and assagai. The bow may prove very important in tracing the origins of the human race. There seems to have been a great watershed on one side of which every one knew the bow, while on the other, side it was unknown.

There is a Zoo here which is an unworthy place, but we were interested to see some gnu, or wildebeeste as they call them here, loose in a field. These creatures are dangerous in the rutting season and have killed more than one person who crossed their preserve. This information induced my two lads to instantly climb the fence and wait to see what would happen, but apparently it was not the rutting season, as beyond kicking up the dust the creatures showed no sign of displeasure. Beyond the Zoo is a delightful Botanical Gardens full of wild plants and extending right up the mountain-side. Cape Town is the most marvellous place for wild flowers, and a friend told me that in September he had picked 147 different sorts in a single morning. We were especially interested in the groves of silver trees, which grow nowhere else in the world, and will not bear transplanting. It is a fair-sized tree, 20 or 30 feet high, with velvety leaves, silvery on the lower side. Why it should only grow here is one of the many mysteries of nature.

On November 21st I got down to business at the City Hall with an audience of 1,750. There was no seat vacant. They listened with indulgence if not with acquiescence. Then I called for written questions. Presently I had such a pile before me that I remarked to my audience, "We are here for the night!" On the whole they were a sensible lot of queries on familiar lines and I had no difficulty in dealing with them. Some of them made the audience laugh. "If the other world is so pleasant, why don't you all commit suicide?" I had to explain what a serious offence this is and how formidable the consequences. "*Must* I have the same husband?" asked several. I relieved their minds by explaining that when there was no sympathy there was no reunion. How amazing it is that all this definite vital information should have been coming through for eighty years and that folk should still be so ignorant. I wonder if newspaper editors and proprietors have any inkling of the responsibility which they have incurred, or what it will mean to them hereafter. Remorse – deep, deep remorse.

My experience was by no means so happy two days later when I lectured at Stellenbosch. This place is the centre of the Dutch Reformed Church, one of the more unprogressive sects, and word had been passed round that so dangerous a heretic was not to be encouraged. The small British colony turned up in force, but there was hardly a Dutchman in the Hall, though the Mayor bravely took the chair. Sometimes quality makes up for quantity and you never know the upshot. It was worth doing if only for the view of a glorious rainbow which spanned the whole Northern sky, and through which we seemed to drive as we approached the town. It seemed symbolical of the doctrine of hope which we were carrying to this centre of narrow sectarian bigotry.

The Dutch and British feeling is certainly very strong, and is hardly controlled by their mutual fear of the native. The political situation is that the Diehard Dutch, who in a mild way are Republicans, allied themselves with Labour so that the Coalition could have a majority. They call themselves Nationalists, but the Labour men are mostly British. These people now run the country. The Opposition is strong, however, and is led by Smuts, who is far the biggest man in South Africa. He calls his party the South African party, and the British are all at his back, together with the greater number of the more moderate and educated Dutch. The Opposition has only a minority of fifteen in the House and it has a majority in the Senate, so that the Nationalists are not in a strong position. There is no doubt that these people do not want a British immigration into this country, and do what they can to prevent it.

To-day (November 24th) I went over the two Houses of Parliament and examined the library which, under the loving care of Mr. Ribbink, the chief librarian, is a really remarkable collection. So far as Africana are concerned it is no doubt unique in the world. Among many other relics they treasure particularly the table on which King Edward at Windsor signed the Act of Union. The pen, with the ink still carefully preserved upon it, lies beside it. No doubt, like Rizzio's blood, the ink will from time to time be renewed.

We held a séance in our sitting-room yesterday, the medium being a Mrs. Kimpton, of whom I had heard good things. We had our good friends the Ashton Jonsons there, and also several new inquirers into the subject, including the wife of the Dutch administrator of the Colony, the wife of the Swiss Consul, a leading doctor and his wife, and finally Miss Zena Dare, the well-known London actress, who is playing in *The Trial of Mary Dugan* at the local theatre.

Our results were excellent. After going into trance the medium took each person in turn and gave conclusive evidential messages, accompanied by correct names, from those who had passed on. One lady who had greatly loved a little white dog was told that such a dog was frisking round her, trying to lick her hand. Miss Dare received some evidential matter which claimed to be from Ellen Terry. In an hour of incessant talking I do not think that Mrs. Kimpton made more than two or three mistakes as to facts, which is fewer than one might make if one was an intermediate between two living

beings. Altogether it was a very convincing dispjay, dignified and uplifting. All the novices seemed to be much
impressed, though, as usual, rather dazed with the new
knowledge.

Psychic phenomena do certainly take most extraordinary forms. In the evening the Ashton Jonsons and I
went to test the powers of a Mrs. Butters, who was said
upon occasion to be controlled and used by a great
Italian opera singer named Sabatini. The performance
was certainly a notable one. The lady had musical
powers of her own which were expressed originally in a
high coloratura soprano, gradually lowering to a mezzo,
and finally developing into a contralto. She spoke no
Italian, though she had once learned to sing "Caro mio
ben." We waited in semidarkness, seven or eight of us,
for half an hour or more. Then suddenly she rose,
apparently in deep trance, struck a dramatic attitude and
began singing, "Lascia chio, pianga" in a fine full baritone voice, a good five notes, as her husband assured us,
below the lowest she could possibly take. She sang for
about ten minutes, and Ashton Jonson, who is a musical
critic of note and the author of the *Handbook to
Chopin's Works*, assured me that the voice was not only
undoubtedly male but of exceptional quality. It had that
note of agony in its higher passages which I have
observed and resented in Caruso, which is, I presume, a
peculiarity of the Italian school. The Italian words came

fluently. Then suddenly the song stopped and I heard the singer cry, "Basta! Basta!" (Enough! Enough!) A few minutes later the lady recovered from her trance and complained of pain and discomfort of her larynx, as if it had been unduly stretched. We surmised that it was a consciousness of this which had caused the Italian control to cut his performance short.

What are we to say of such a performance as that? I do not readily ascribe things to psychic causes if there can be any normal explanation. Personally I can see none. There is no question of the honesty of those concerned, and the universal testimony was that the lady neither kmew Italian nor that particular piece of music. This is more conclusive than the voice, as I have known women who could sing baritone and even bass, though not of so splendid and unforced a quality. As a fact this lady, Mrs. Butters, has many other mediumistic powers, including that of apports, so that we must judge the singing as simply one of her psychic gifts and the control as a true one. She is also controlled at times by an African girl who speaks the language of clicks, and claims to have been educated or converted by Dr. Livingstone. Not knowing the language of clicks, I was unable to test this control.

My wife's tender heart is much concerned by the condition of the animals here, the horses, and mules being worked when very old and emaciated. The drivers, who are usually Kaffirs, lash them unmercifully and are generally brutal. It is said to be even worse on the farms, where the horses are literally worked to death. My wife has written a splendid letter to the *Argus*, straight from her heart. She did the same, I remember, over bearing-reins in Washington, and effected, I believe, some improvement.

On Sunday, November 25th, it was determined that we should show the assembled citizens of Cape Town, in their Town Hall assembled, what a well-conducted Spiritualistic service is like. The result was amazing. The proceedings were to begin at 8.15, but at six o'clock the people were at the doors. When we arrived 3,000 people were packed into the Hall, and many of the chief people in the town were unable to get seats. I saw with regret the wife of the Administrator, Mrs. Fourie, a very charming Dutch lady, Miss Zena Dare and other friends standing among the crowd. Mr. Ashton Jonson was in the chair, and read beautifully the chapter from Corinthians about the gifts of the Spirit, and the noble passages about charity. The hymns were perfectly chosen and well sung, including "The world has felt a quickening breath," which was written by a factory girl in Manchester, named Lily Doten, under control, and is one of the finest hymns in words and music in our language. My own address seemed to get across. I said that I had felt lonely of late and could wish that those would stand up who had enjoyed the same experiences as I had described. About a quarter of the audience sprang to their feet. I also read them a long message from Pheneas, part of which had been specially given for that meeting. Finally I read an account of the Christ given by one who had met Him on the farther side. As the address was broadcasted, I hope it may have brought a wave of new thought and broader vision to many isolated folk.

On the Monday night I gave my photographic lecture, with the Hall crammed once more. The effect of such an exhibition is curious. Our Press has succeeded so completely in misrepresenting the subject during the last fifty years, that people are quite unprepared for a direct and undeniable demonstration. At first one is conscious of an atmosphere of curiosity mingled with incredulity; but as proof follows proof, and they see Crookes' own photographs of a materialized spirit, Geley's photographs of semi-materialized spirit, the ectoplasm of various mediums, the testimony of plate manufacturers that the medium never had access to the plates, and other such demonstrations, it is awe which submerges all other emotions. This was the lecture which I had to repeat eight times, in New York, and I could certainly have filled the Cape Town City Hall several times, but my dates would not allow.

I have been fairly occupied, for besides the lectures, the sightseeing, the incessant interviews, the social hospitalities and keeping this record up to date, I have had the usual brisk newspaper contention in the two big papers, the *Argus* and *Cape Times*. It is curious that the attacks come from two entirely opposite sources, the one being the Materialist who resents the idea of an after life, the other the ultra-religious four-square blockhead – I know no other name for him – who maintains that every word of the Bible, including such precepts as "Be not good over-much" or "The dead know not anything," is inspired. One would wish to slip out of the fight altogether, and let these two settle it between themselves.

And now our days in this beautiful city have drawn to a close. We could not possibly have had a happier, a busier, or a more successful fortnight, and save for the south-east winds we found the place itself to be ideal in its climate. Our next pitch is to be Port Elizabeth, and after all had been paid and the reservations made we find at the last instant that great gales and heavy rain which have occurred lately have undermined the railway and that all our plans are literally a "wash-out." However, it so happened that the *Armadale Castle* was just starting for the same port, and so it is that I sit at the present moment on the deck in the sunlight with my wife and Billy beside me, having a quiet day and watching the distant panorama of the hilly coast of the Eastern Province. To-morrow early (November 29th) we reach Port Elizabeth and I lecture on the same night.

REINCARNATION

We had a chat upon deck under the light of the stars upon the complex subject of reincarnation. If we disagree upon it, it is at least a noble philosophic subject for disagreement, and not a petty point of dogma. Personally I have never been clear upon the point, and am inclined to think that with the more advanced souls incarnation may be optional. One story vouched for by Mr. Ashton Jonson was about a friend who had a very clear recollection that he had been killed at Waterloo, and also that he had been a member of White's Club. He remembered his old name. On looking up the records of the Club the name was duly found. I should not regard this as conclusive, but at least it is very suggestive. Another passenger was warned by a seer – a Rhodesian policeman, of all professions – that he had wronged a comrade in a former incarnation, that this comrade was now reincarnated and was near him and would have his revenge by a similar wrong done to him. Sure enough, he went into partnership with a friend and was badly swindled by him, and only afterwards got information which thoroughly identified the criminal with the description given by the seer. It seems a bleak prospect if a man in hundreds of years cannot forget but will carry a feud on into a new incarnation. It does not seem as if the teaching of the Spheres had made him a better man.

Late into the night we talked upon high topics with

the Cape Aguilas light sliding slowly from our port bow to our quarter and then twinkling far astern. The Cape Town adventure was happily done. The Port Elizabeth experience lay before us. Meanwhile the great dark circle of ocean and the mighty canopy of stars soothed our minds and gave us promise of that mighty peace when all our little human activities are at last at rest and our work will have found its end.

CHAPTER III

Port Elizabeth – A Liberal Rabbi – "The Garden of Death" –
The Strange Canoe –Port Elizabeth – Reminiscences of 1900
– Political Misunderstanding – The Bywoner – Sanna's Post –
Maritzburg – I Meet Several Friends – The Voortrekkers – A
Spirit Dog.

When we reached the deck upon the morning of
Thursday, November 28th, we had already dropped
anchor, and the magnificent panorama of Algoa Bay lay
before our eyes, with Port Elizabeth as a crescent of
white-walled, red-roofed houses extending round the
centre of it. It is certainly a beautiful town, as seen from
the sea, and it promises to be a very prosperous one, for
it is one of the most progressive places in the Union, and
is likely to be the industrial centre of the future. Its present white population, predominantly British, is 29,000,
with about as many coloured folk in attendance.

We had heard that it was less backward than most
cities in psychic things, and this became evident as our
tender approached the quay, for a group of people, who
must have got up early to welcome us, waved their hats
and handkerchiefs, and gave a loud cheer as we came

alongside. When we had clambered up the steps they surrounded us with smiling faces and outstretched hands. There were no Christian clergymen among our welcomers, which is not surprising, but what was both surprising and gratifying was to find that the Jewish Rabbi, Mr. Levy, had joined the deputation. It was a fine public sign that the broad universal appeal of our movement was getting across to the public. In conversation I found that he was a deep student of the subject, and that he was intellectually convinced, although he had never had any psychic experience himself. This is, of course, a perfectly logical attitude, but how rare it is! The average "scientific" man's view is as absurd as if a man denied the testimony about aerolites because he had never himself seen one fall.

I found, with a little dismay, that a lady, Mrs. Lucy Smith, had been chosen to fill the chair at the evening lecture. I have a horror of the chairman who anticipates my argument or irritates my audience by taking for granted that which should be proved. My companion, Ashton Jonson, makes an ideal chairman, so that I should have felt safe in his hands. However, I may say at once that Mrs. Lucy Smith did splendidly in the evening. She has that rare thing in women, an audible voice in public speaking, and her appearance is pleasing and sympathetic, so that I had no reason to regret the local choice.

When the reception was over we drove out to the Humewood Hotel, which has a most lovely view of the sea from its front windows. As I write in our sitting-room the line of creaming surf is right beneath me. Then come all those wonderful shades, light bottle-green, dark bottle-green, light blue, and then the huge expanse of darker blue with purple patches to mark the shadows. It was a bright sunlit day and the outlook was an exquisite one – an omen of success.

We set off at once to see the Snake Park, which is the show place of the town. Its existence is entirely due to the remarkable qualities of Mr. Fitzsimmons, who, with his no less remarkable wife, has originated and carried out this extraordinary undertaking. He is a man some forty-five years of age, but looking younger than his years, keen, alert, with all the stigmata of genius. I was delighted to find that both he and his wife were well acquainted with psychic truth. Mrs. Fitzsimmons showed me a psychic photograph of her husband taken by Hope of Crew, upon which a really beautiful portrait of her own dead sister had appeared over the sitter.

We viewed the snakes with a very necessary small parapet for our protection. There in a sunken garden, with a little watercourse running round it, were snakes of every sort, snakes dark and green, and brown and red, snakes sleeping, snakes wriggling, snakes rearing and, most graceful of all, snakes swimming, beautiful undulating lines of green and yellow in the clear waterway which ran round the garden. There was the dark mamba, who kills in twenty minutes, the terrible yellow cobra, and the dark chequered puff adder with its loathsome head. "The Garden of Death" would be a fit name for such a place.

Then an amazing person put in an appearance. He was a sturdy negro, coal-black, with a jolly, smiling face. He wore gloves and high leggings. This sportsman lowered himself into the pit and proceeded to take all manner of liberties with its occupants. Of course he knew which were harmless, and only proceeded to extremes with those; but none the less he walked with perfect unconcern among the rearing creatures, the cobras and mambas, who pecked at his gaiters. He has already been bitten thirteen times, and the last one would have been fatal had it not been for the prompt ministration of Mr. Fitzsimmons, who has prepared a snake serum which is a specific against any bite. In view of our further journeys, and the snake-hunting habits of our lads, we thought it wise to purchase a complete outfit – lancet, syringe, and antidote – so as to ensure us against accidents. We were then all photographed handling snakes, which I need not say were *not* cobras and mambas.

They are queer creatures, snakes, and you never quite know how they will act. In this Park they all live, big and little, in perfect amity. You see them writhing across each other in complete brotherhood. There would seem to be nothing inherently cruel or vicious in their nature. Some time ago Mr. Fitzsimmons put a number of rats into the enclosure where his pythons lay. In the morning it was found that the rats had killed four of the pythons. It seemed as if the big sleepy creatures were so insensible that they had never felt the little brutes, who were gnawing holes in their torpid bodies.

Fitzsimmons is one of those men of genius who illuminate everything they touch. He is also a fine organizer, which is by no means a common property of genius. The little local museum has been built up by his exertions. Apart from his snake toxine, which is known all over Africa, he has made experiments which have convinced him that his snake fluid is a complete cure for epilepsy. He has records of many cases, and his argument is a strong one; but he complains that because he is not a certified medical man he is not allowed to put his views forward in the technical journals or meetings. This seems a very serious charge and should certainly be inquired into. The observations of such a man are too valuable to many sufferers for any suppression.

Mr. Fitzsimmons told me one remarkable story. Some years ago a dug-out canoe came drifting into Algoa Bay. It was naturally supposed to be some native African craft which had been abandoned. Mr. Fitzsimmons examined it, however, and concluded that it was of some wood which did not exist in Africa. He sent a specimen cut from the canoe to Oxford, and the expert opinion was that the wood was Javan or Sumatran. Thus this frail craft had been carried by wind and current right across the whole Indian Ocean, just as the logs of Columbus were carried across the Atlantic.

There are sharks upon this coast so they have railed off a splendid swimming-place where the great rollers come in very much as we have seen them do at Manly, near Sydney. I went down to see Mr. Ashton Jonson and Billy disporting themselves, and would very gladly have joined them; but, alas! no bathing-dress could be found which corresponded with my measurements.

We found the Opera House crammed in the evening, and all went well. The proceedings had a charming opening, for a dear old Spiritualist, over eighty years of age, came upon the platform and made us a presentation of a very fine silver jackal kaross – a really splendid gift. His kindly words were even more welcome than the beautiful rug, which was fit to adorn a palace. I am told that the élite of the town and district were among my audience and I was conscious of a very liberal atmosphere. They applauded loudly when I said that the Rabbi had met me, and even more when I refused to accept a text as an argument, adding that there was no text in the Bible which had not some other text to contradict it. The questions were of a very intelligent nature, though occasionally they wandered into the grotesque, as when one man wanted to know whether there were flats in heaven. I answered that we had authority for many mansions, but that I could not give any more detailed information. There was a great pile of questions, so that although it was 8.15 when I began I did not finish till 10.20. I was tired, but not exhausted. Altogether it was a most successful evening.

The next morning was spent in exploring the beauties of Port Elizabeth, which are many. We drove to Shoenmaker's Point, which is a really lovely seascape about 10 miles out. The whole drive was a dream of beauty. The boys went off in the morning to visit a friend, Mr. George Clarke, who had a fruit (orange) and dairy farm about 30 miles out. There they had a day full of exciting adventures, and turned up mudstained and radiant at one of the local stations on the way to Bloemfontein. They tell us, though it was hard for us to believe, not only that there are many monkeys in the hinterland, but that there is a bit of thick scrub, almost impenetrable to man, within a few miles of Mr. Clarke's farm at Addo in which there is still to be found a herd of elephants, which are protected partly by the scrub and partly by their own ferocity. I confess I never dreamed that heavy game could be found wild so near a large civilized city.

The late evening saw us off to Bloemfontein. The station platform was crowded with dear warm-hearted souls who had assembled to give us a parting cheer, which they very literally and loudly did. It was pleasant to carry away the memory of their happy, smiling faces.

It was a tiring journey to the capital of the Orange Free State and took us just twenty-six hours, so that we were weary folk when late at night on December 1st we found ourselves in Polley's Hotel. Travelling is not luxurious in South Africa – it is leather, not velvet – but all that any reasonable man could wish is to be found. Occasionally there is a plague of insects, but we were not molested much. It is recorded that one traveller, who had been badly bitten, sent a fierce complaint to the management, and received so courteous and conciliatory a letter in reply that he was quite soothed, until by chance a memorandum which was there fell out of the envelope, and he read: "Send this guy our bug letter."

Much came back to me from the long ago as we sped over the veld in the gloaming, and the lights of Bloemfontein began to gleam on the horizon. It had been a wonderful sunset. A dull line of crimson smouldered along the horizon. Above it was an expanse of delicate apple-green, shot with those long dark clouds of evening which are the most gently melancholy of all Nature's trappings. The apple-green deepened into dark blue and that into a rich purple, in the midst of which

Venus was shining most brilliantly. Around in the half-light one saw the great plain and the loom of fantastic kopjes. Where were all the good fellows who had passed this way with me before, the whole train pulsating with vitality, when from every watch-fire that we passed came the cry, "Who are you?" and the chorus crashed back, "It's the Camerons." That noble battalion had come up with our hospital. Both they and we left many behind us. They fought the Boers and we the enteric, and I don't know which was the more deadly.

We spent our first morning in Bloemfontein in going over some of my old haunts. We drove up an eminence which overlooks the town, and it was clear to me how greatly the place has increased and prospered. Then we went down to the Ramblers' ground, where a beautiful smooth cricket field lies where our mud-infested hospital was pitched. The great pavilion room, which formed our chief room, and in which I have seen many a good man die, was the same as ever, with its inane little stage at one end, where the scenery of H.M.S. *Pinafore* gave a macabre touch to the horrible scenes which I have witnessed in that room. Thence we were taken to see two monuments, one of which commemorates the struggles of the brave burghers with the Kaffirs.

The other monument has at its base the graves of General de Wet and President Steyne, both of them good and brave men, before whom I gladly bared my head. On examining the inscription upon the monument, however, I found that it commemorated the 26,000 women and children who died in the Concentration Camps, and it seemed to me, so far as I could interpret the Dutch, that it placed the blame of this upon the British. I therefore protested to the Dutch journalist who had taken us round that this was false, and that such an assertion was disgraceful. He made no attempt to enlighten me as to the real meaning of the inscription, which I was assured afterwards was not meant to be offensive, but he published an interview next day in the *Volksblad*, which is the chief Dutch paper, in which it would appear that I had gone out of my way to attack the monument, as if the women and children had no right to such a thing. There was considerable excitement in the town, and indeed I do not wonder, though the whole thing was founded half upon misapprehension and half upon misrepresentation.

On the morning after the interview appeared I called upon the editor of the *Volksblad*, the paper which had published it. I found him to be a very courteous gentleman, who listened with attention to my account and that of Ashton Jonson, which put the matter in its true light. He said that the inscription was in Afrikaans, not in Dutch, and that I had misunderstood it, and that there was no intention to cast any reflection on any one. I answered that in that case my own remarks were made under a regrettable misapprehension, but I pointed out that the Dutch journalist who was the cause of the trouble should have apprised me of my error. I drew up a letter which embodied the result of our conversation. This, however, could not appear till next day, and Dutch citizens were unaware of the change in the situation. The result was that in the afternoon a so-called commando of some hundreds of young men assembled outside the hotel with threats of violence. We were away upon a long motor drive to the Brandford Plain, and by the time we returned these people had been dispersed by the police. There were threats directed against us, and friends even went the length of advising us to join the train next day at the first station down the line. This of course was unthinkable, and we were in no way molested next morning. Reports of this matter were forwarded to England, and did not come to my eyes for months afterwards, which might give the entirely false impression that I had retracted my opinion in the face of mob violence. This, as I have here shown, is entirely false, as the demonstration occurred hours after the explanation.

I was pretty sure of my ground in this matter, as I had examined the facts at the time. In the latter part of the war all the cattle had been rounded up, and even the abounding game upon the veld had all been shot, some by the Boers and some by the British. The guerrilla war had broken out, and it was necessary to concentrate all males, since it was impossible to tell the fighting Boer from the harmless farmer. This being so the women and children in isolated farms were not only in danger of starvation, but had no protection against Kaffir attacks. The British Government under these circumstances could not leave these poor people to perish, so they gathered them into camps near the railway lines where food could be provided. It was an extraordinary act of clemency by which we fought the husbands while we fed the wives. Unhappily there came an epidemic of enteric, measles and scarlatina which ravaged the whole country and took a heavy toll of the camps – though I believe the figures of mortality were quite as high in the towns. That under these circumstances an enduring monument should cause perpetual bitterness by putting the blame on the British would be an intolerable thing and one which one could not pass without protest; but since I am assured that no such accusation was meant, all is well.

There were many repercussions from this political incident at Bloemfontein. The *Cape Argus*, in a rather feeble leader, described my action as "tactless", but there is a point where tact and cowardice can hardly be distinguished, and surely that point has been reached if a Briton can look upon an inscription which appears to him to insult and defame his own country, and yet utters no protest. That is not the tradition of our race. On the other hand if, as the editor of the *Volksblad* assured me, the inscription was harmless, why then of course my protest was made under a misconception which was encouraged by the Dutch journalist at my elbow. It became clear to me, however, after the episode that many of the British took the same view of the monument that I had done and had been equally misled as to the inscription. One of the most respected of the British inhabitants of the town wrote to me:

"May I, without presumption, thank you for speaking out about that miserable 'monument of Hate' which disfigures this town and helps to keep alive the racial hatred that is the curse and infirmity of South Africa."

There was a good deal of abuse of me in some National papers. This did not hurt me at all, but it did apparently stir up the conscience of some of their own people. I had, for instance, the following letter:

"Dear Sir, –

"As a Dutch-speaking South African and a strong Nationalist, I wish you to know that I consider the insults hurled at you, as quite unwarranted and uncalled for.

Having read your works and knowing your feelings towards humanity in general, I for one need no assurance from you that there was no intention of hurting any section of the community. The despicable remarks in *ons Vaderland* should be treated with the contempt they deserve. To attack your mission in South Africa in such a way seems to me beyond the bounds of common decency. To reach that stage one must be saturated with ulcers of malice. You may make use of this letter if you think fit."

Apparently I might use the name, but it would be an ill service to my kind correspondent.

One thing I will say, in conclusion, to my Dutch friends, and that is that if I had read an inscription erected by Britons and reflecting upon the humanity of the Boers, so as to cause racial feeling, I would have protested with equal warmth.

In the evening we filled two motors and went a 20-mile journey to Sanna's Post, where Q battery was cut up and Hornby got his V.C. I had a very vivid recollection of my last visit there, when the dead horses still marked the position of the guns. All was quite unchanged, and the driver of one of the motors had been one of De Wet's men upon that occasion, so we had the story from the other side. The old Waterworks were still standing. I have always thought that the one blot upon Lord Roberts's South African campaign was that he did not strike out eastward at once and recover his cut water supply. We lost more by disease than by the bullet, and it was that unfortunate omission which increased our losses. I can hardly believe that this clean, fresh, healthy town is the hell-hole of old, which could be smelt many miles before you saw it, and where we buried as many as sixty men a day.

We passed one dramatic figure on the way out – a white man dressed in rags like a Kaffir, with a fierce, energetic face, crisp yellow beard, blue eyes, and the figure of Adonis. He stands for a difficult problem – that of the landless Boer. He is the disinherited one, the grandson of the men who conquered the land, now by the freak of fate left without a yard of land for himself. He is the bywoner, the backveld Boer, ignorant perhaps, but virile and capable, a hunter, a fighter. His elder brothers have the farm. There is no capital to buy another. What is he to do? Out of this stuff come the Voortrekkers, the Angola Boers, the Stellaland pioneers, and all the other strange twigs which grow out of the old Dutch tree. They are splendid fellows, and it is a cruel fate which places us now and then in opposition.

In spite of our political misadventure our Spiritual mission at Bloemfontein seems to have been eminently successful. We had many messages and letters to prove it. I cannot refrain from quoting one which said: "It was a wonderful experience in this materialistic age to form part of an audience of over 2,000 listening spellbound for two hours or more to a sermon preached, not in a church, but in a theatre, on the subject of the immortality of the soul. Many who came to scoff remained to pray. I could not help thinking of a Biblical parallel: 'Now when they heard of the resurrection of the dead, some mocked; but, others said, We will hear thee again on this matter.' "

These are the things that help one on one's way.

At the last moment before starting I saw Leonard Flemming, who has the qualities of a considerable writer – a short, strong brown man of middle age. His work should be better known in England, and is essential to anyone who thinks of settling here upon the land. It is to be remembered, however, that Flemming is Australian born and has helped to run a bush farm from the time he could walk, so that much might be possible to him which would be impossible for the average emigrant.

Besides Flemming I met several men whom I was glad to know in the capital of the O.F.S. There was a fine Wesleyan clergyman, a Welshman named Frank Edwards, who in spite of his cloth joined as a private in 1914 and was soon at the head of his company. He told me that on one occasion in France his dead mother had suddenly appeared in a vision before him, had led him by the hand out of his dugout, and that the said dugout had fallen in immediately afterwards. How many stories of the sort exist and how strange that people should sneer at the only scheme of philosophy which can explain them!

Another outstanding figure was General Grobler, a man of very distinguished appearance, and the Administrator of the State. He commanded the Boers at the battle of Stormberg, and gave me a very interesting account of the action. Gatacre's attack was very well managed and a complete surprise. The Boers on the hill were on the point of surrendering when Grobler came up with 300 mounted men *behind* two British guns which were raking the hill. He charged these guns, got into them almost before the gunners saw him, and so saved the situation. He was himself wounded and, taken by the British shortly afterwards. What with Smuts and Hertzog, Fourie and Grobler, the whole country seems to be governed now by the men who gave us most trouble thirty years ago – and a fine lot of men they are.

As our train left for Natal in the morning of December 6th we met another which brought in General Smuts, who was to preside over a general congress of the South African party. The more one sees of South African politics the more one admires Smuts. He is a really great man, and if the country solidifies the credit and glory will be his. He works always as an African for Africa, but his Africa is a united land where Boer and British are as brothers. His opponents, the Nationalists, headed by Hertzog, have the narrower conception of a country predominantly Dutch. Their argument is a clear one, and if we were of their blood we would appreciate it. It is *their* land, they say. They founded it, they extended it. They conquered the wilderness and the savage. They moved on and on in order to avoid the British. And now after all they are part of the Empire. It is a light yoke, if a yoke at all, but it is a restless, spirited creature which bears it. But facts are facts, and Smuts will win in the long run, though I see, since my return home, that the Nationalists have a clear majority at the 1929 election.

All day on December 5th we have been crossing the extraordinarily fertile plain which separates Bloemfontein from Natal. It is a marvellous sea of green and yellow, with occasional coffee-coloured streaks where the sun-dried dongas gape.

At long intervals are the cosy white homes peeping out of their green nests of eucalyptus. And all over this huge gently undulating plain rise the isolated fantastic kopjes, castellated, battlemented, and grotesquely wonderful. I bought a pamphlet on the geology of the country at the Cape Town Museum, but it helps me very little, for these scientific men never seem to realize that unlearned people like myself can make nothing of their eternal jargon, and so I read this through and never once found any rational explanation of the one obvious question which demands an answer from every one who looks at the country with eyes which have a brain behind them – namely, how came the kopjes to be there, a formation unlike anything else in the world, and extending over a thousand miles. The nearest that I can get to it is that the level of the kopjes was the original level of the whole great sandy plain, that the said plain was all lowered in its level by wind and rain and dust storms, and that the hard knobbly bits did not dissolve so quickly – though they are obviously dissolving – and so remain thrusting their queer bulk out of the sunken plain. That explanation will have to do for me until I get a better one.

It is a marvellous change from the high veld where we were yesterday, to the lush semi-tropical vegetation of Natal, which we entered this morning. We arrived at Maritzburg at 5.30 a.m., and even at that deadly hour found Mr. Mason and other local Spiritualists on the platform, while Mr. Etellin, the very capable manager of the Imperial Hotel, came down also to welcome us. His establishment is a very comfortable one, and will be even more so in the future, as he is building: a large annexe upon most modern lines. One could not be better housed.

Mr. Mason, an ardent Spiritualist and ex-mayor of the town, took the chair for me in the evening at the Town Hall at an excellent meeting, which I hope did good. The great heat was against a full house, but it was a remarkable gathering all the same. I had spent the day in going round the city, which is a very alert and prosperous place with 25,000 inhabitants. It is so situated among what one might call the foothills of the high veld, that its elevation of 1,800 feet makes it an intermediate point for those either above or below who desire a climate change. We are alarmed, however, to think that Durban should be hotter, for this is as much as one can reasonably be asked to endure. I alleviated it by two swims, but even so it was the limit.

There is an excellent Museum here, with some fine specimens of Bushman paintings. What intrigued me most, however, was a coin found in digging out some foundations. It is undoubtedly a bronze of ancient Judea with the usual chalice mark, and dating from about 200 B.C. By what possible means did such a thing get to Natal – by barter, by shipwreck, or how? It would be an excellent subject for a good psychometrist.

The Museum which interested me most, however, was the Voortrekker Museum, which contained the relics of the early Boer pioneers, which in many ways reminded us of the Mormon relics in Salt Lake City. To begin with, there was a tilted wagon, exactly like the prairie schooners with which Brigham Young crossed the plains. But the most interesting part was the collection of old flintlocks and elephant guns with which these extraordinary men conquered the Zulus. There were pictures too which made one realize that remarkable episode in history which may perhaps justify a paragraph of digression.

In 1835 was the great trek of Boer farmers from the Cape, thousands of them passing North in order to avoid British rule, which had never been welcome and was now aggravated by the abolition of slavery, which was thought to be both beneficial and moral by these Old Testament Puritans. They wandered on, and at last in 1838 one diverging stream of them came pouring down the passes into Northern Natal – long lines of ox-drawn wagons crammed with women and children, guarded by a cloud of mounted men. At that very moment Great Britain had extended her sway to South Natal and had taken Port Natal, afterwards Durban, so that after all their struggles the Boers found themselves once more face to face with that which they were striving to avoid. Natal at the time was practically depopulated, for the terrible Panda, the son of Chaka, had come down with his fierce tribesmen and killed all life, save a few cowering creatures in the kloofs of the mountains. It seemed to the Boers that Dingaan, who had assassinated and then succeeded Panda, was now the legitimate owner by right of conquest, and therefore they hastened to get a legal grant from him. Piet Retief, their leader, with seventy men, went up to Dingaan's kraal, to get the precious document which would secure their position as against the British. Dingaan persuaded them to leave horses and guns outside the kraal, and then murdered them all. There is a very powerful pen-and-ink sketch in the Museum where you see Dingaan, with a fiendish face, suddenly springing up and stabbing in the air with his assagai as a sign for the slaughter, while the horrified, indignant, expostulating faces of the Boers are admirably depicted.

The next act of the drama was even more terrible. The Zulus at once swept down upon the unprepared laagers, murdering every one they met. Six hundred perished. To this day the district is called Weenen, the place of tears.

And then comes the splendid third act, when the villain is foiled as villains should be. These brave fellows gathered themselves together and awaited the Zulu attack. They formed their wagons four-square with iron chains between and their families and possessions in the centre. Thus by steady nerves and good shooting out of these very same old guns which I handled to-day they gave the Zulus such a mauling that the place is called Blood River to this day. It was exactly what the British did at Rorke's Drift forty years later, and in each case it was a magnificent exploit, and in the Blood River episode it was the first time that the magnificent and disciplined Zulu ever learned that there was something upon earth which was stronger than himself. They were terrible and wonderful men, these Voortrekkers. There is the leather breeches of one of them hung in the Museum which could not have been less than 60 inches on the waist-line, and yet it is hard to think that a Voortrekker could be fat. That man was surely a giant.

Just one psychic anecdote before we plunge into Durban. A staid and sober citizen of good repute told me this story after my lecture. His little girl was going to school and was assaulted by a Kaffir lad. A dog sprang out, attacked the boy, who bolted, and then escorted the child home. All the family, including the narrator, patted its head and fondled it. Then before their eyes it dematerialized. It was half-Airedale, half-Irish terrier, and did not correspond to any dog they had lost or to any neighbour's dog. It is easy to explain such a story on the grounds of lies, but surely the time has come when the world has become more wise, for many other such examples could be given. The child of course would be mediumistic, and the control (whom Catholics would call the Guardian Angel) would work the materialization. There are no miracles, and it all comes back to natural law but dimly understood.

CHAPTER IV

Durban – The Valley of a Thousand Hills – Abduhl Latif, an Evidential Case – A Durban Séance – Dick King – The Protection of Natives – Denis makes his Debut – The Zulu Seer – Glorious Bathing – The East Indian Problem.

We reached Durban on the evening of Friday, December 7th, after a 60-mile motor drive of remarkable beauty. In parts the country is very like England, but a mountain range, 2,500 feet high, has to be crossed, and the road, which seemed to me to be a remarkable piece of engineering, shows wonderful prospects at every turn both in the ascent and the descent. The curves are terrific and a driver must go slow with good brakes or he will never drive again, for many a good car has crashed down that fearful slope. One man left his wife and three children in a standing Ford while he went to get a tin of water. When he returned there was no car there. It had gone backward down that awful abyss. However, our two cars were safely piloted down by the Walsh brothers, who are the local representatives of the great firm of Williams, Hunt & Co., who have made up by their private courtesy for any coldness we have had from the Government. Perhaps it is that we were spoiled by Canadian kindness and so expected too much from official South Africa.

Half-way across the hills our cars were halted to enable us to look down into a tremendous side valley which stretched away to the horizon, where it ended in a row of flat-topped ranges. This is the famous Valley of a Thousand Hills, which is a noted beauty spot, but only as a distant view, for few penetrate into its mystery and there are no roads down there. In this strange wilderness, we are told, there are at least 20,000 natives, broken clans, Pondos and Zulus, self-supporting in their mealie patches and seldom visible to the white population. It seems a strange neighbour for a great civilized city, and I was informed by one who has explored this vastness that every man down there has his shield, his assagai and his knobkerry. However, if the Bolshevists leave them alone, there is no present danger from the natives.

Our first impression of Durban was one of surprised admiration. We did not expect to find so splendid a town, with broad streets, great public buildings, fine hotels, and every amenity. Our own particular hostel was the Marine Hotel, which overlooks the bay, and is as comfortable a place as we have encountered in our travels, save only the Mount Nelson. The excellent East

Indian servants, quick, silent and alert, give a service such as few European towns can boast of. They are queer, inscrutable fellows. One of them came into my room just now with some earnest request, which he made in so low and ingratiating a voice that I, who grow deafer, could make nothing of it. At first I thought he wanted to be paid for a newspaper and then that he was charging for notepaper, but finally, with my wife's aid, I discovered that he represented an Indian paper and that he wanted to draw me. Nothing doing.

Malcolm has gone on to Johannesburg – his first long independent flight – and we were amused to see an interview with him – or extracts from it – in a Durban paper. Some horror was mingled with our amusement. It was headed "Young Doyle seeks the Bright Lights", and it was to the effect that he had come on to Jo'burg because it was the one town that had night clubs, and that its great defect as a town was that it had not a good motor-racing track. The second item gives the correct impression of being a good sportsman, which he undoubtedly is; but the first one, coming from a teetotaller, a vegetarian, and at present a non-smoker, might mislead the reader. It is one of the most pleasing characteristics of the new generation, shared by many besides my own boys, that dancing and other innocent pleasures can be disassociated entirely from alcohol. This was seldom so when I was young, and it is a great advance.

Our party has been reinforced here by the arrival of Mrs. Ashton Jonson from Cape Town. She most nobly allowed her husband to come with us on our land travels, where he has been simply invaluable as a buffer between me and the world. She herself is extraordinarily useful, as her letters in reply to our numerous psychic inquiries are models of what such things should be. So now we have a full team once more and are in even higher heart than when we started.

We have just had what would seem to be an excellent proof of that spirit protection which has been extended to us while we work in this cause. Please note the dates and details. On November 26th Mrs. Court, who is an amateur clairvoyante at Cape Town, wrote as follows:

"I wish to tell Sir Arthur that there was an Eastern Spirit, either Indian or Persian (I am inclined to think Indian), standing near him, not on the platform beside him, but at his feet a little to his left; he was tall and thin, very thin narrow face, high forehead, thin scanty beard, about a foot long; he wore a long white toga, a rolled turban (you will know what I mean, you know the Eastern style of turbans) – a black fez cap; he was by no means grandly clothed; the turban was shabby, as was also the toga; he leaned all the time on a long staff, holding it with both hands; his name is Abdulla. He said 'he' (meaning Sir Arthur) 'long years ago, fed me when I was hungry – I shall never forget – not only with bread,

84

but with better than bread. He still feeds the hungry. I say to him. Be of good cheer, I stand near him to give him strength and courage. I place my hand over his head and give him my blessing; this I have done many times, though he knows it not. The sun of his life shall grow brighter as the daylight fades; in the evening time of his life there shall be a great light. My brother, I greet thee.' In English this sounds dull and flat, but in his Eastern way of saying it, it is literally too beautiful for words. Even if I could give Sir Arthur this message, I don't suppose he would recognize his grateful brother, but I've put it down."

So far so good, but there was nothing evidential. The fact of the figure having apparently a high hat, with the turban rolled round, suggested a Persian rather than an Indian, but beyond that one could not go.

Yesterday, December 8th, I got a letter from my good friend R.H. Saunders in London, dated November 9th. He has for some years been in touch with a high Persian spirit named Abduhl or Abdulla Latif, who was an historical character living in the days of Saladin. Particulars of his advent to the modern world will be found in Saunders' excellent book *Healing by Spirit Agency*. Now, here is an extract from Saunders' letter:

"At 4.30 to-day I sat with Mrs. Roberts Johnson and Hector Munro and some friends were present. We had a capital sitting, and I asked Joe Griffiths, the spirit control, who has undertaken similar work for me in India and Australia, to see how you were. 'Eh!' said Joe. 'Ah'll do summat for thee – ah'll coom back soon' – a pause of probably three minutes ensued, and Joe came back from a flashing visit to you!! 'Eh, he's none too well ah tell thee – an' he wasn't very well when he started.' – 'I quite believe that,' I said, ' but will he be better?' – 'Thee can be sure o' that, for Abduhl Latif's with him now. Eh! he's well looked after. It's supposed to be a rest, but he's a worker, an' he will stick to't. He's goin' to make a lot o' friends over theer an' he'll coom back a better man always.' – 'Where did you find him?' I asked. – 'Eh, I can't tell thee wheer – there was a mint o' water.' "

What is the critic to say to this? So far as the "mint of water" goes, we were of course at that time some days out from Cape Town. This, however, might in a normal way be guessed by the medium. But when we get the same name Abdulla, represented as doing the same thing (giving me vitality for my work) from two entirely independent sources, I think it is pure mental perversity and dishonesty to attribute such a thing to coincidence. We feel that we are closely guarded and that the veil is very thin between us.

As I am on psychic subjects, I may say that I had a sitting yesterday with Mrs. Kelland, whom I found to be an excellent medium. She has not the same facility and accuracy in getting names as Mrs. Kimpton, but she is little inferior to her. She got several names with messages for me, and I was inclined to discount them, since most of them could have been got from *Who's Who?*, but she put any such thoughts to rest by doing the same for Ashton Jonson. She works much in the smaller dorps, and tells me that the interest is universal. Strange if this land of gold should prove to be, as Pheneas said, "a beacon to the human race."

There is a statue to Dick King, portraying most vividly a very weary man upon a very weary horse close to our hotel. I wonder how many people at home ever heard the name of Dick King or know how he saved a British colony. But at least he is known and honoured at the scene of his exploit. It was in 1840 that the Boers nearly pushed us into the sea. The last fort was in danger, and if help did not come soon there would not be a foothold left and the next British landing party would find the coast fringed with Boer sharpshooters. It was at this supreme crisis that King set off for help, and finding that he could not get through the cordon on the land side he swam his horse across the bay and so began a 600-mile ride over rivers and mountains, which he accomplished in nine days. Since the famous ride which brought the news of Elizabeth's death to James there has been no historical ride to touch it, and Paul Revere's was but a morning canter. Best of all it was successful. From Grahamstown news went to Cape Town, reinforcements were hurried up and the fort was saved. Therefore it is that Natalians take off their hats to the memory of Dick King.

There is another Durban statue about which I would say a word. It is the War Memorial. At present it is very nearly being the best that I have seen, and yet it is spoiled by an intrusion which could be removed to-morrow. The trouble with statues is that while a book can be destroyed or a picture concealed, no one seems to have power to change a statue when once it is up, as we have discovered with the Rima atrocity in Hyde Park. Here in Durban we have a Cenotaph on familiar Lutyen lines with a noble inscription, and the addition of a dead soldier in bronze lying at the base, with a light forever shining over him. That is perfection. You cannot beat it. But, alas! the sculptor has tried to beat it by placing a large group made in Egyptian fashion of porcelain or faience, which covers the front of the simple stonework with garish blue or yellow, and depicts two angels bearing the man's soul aloft, with a dove above for the conventional Holy Ghost, and a starry sky above that. This is all very bold and unusual, but it is unnecessary and an intrusion. If even now some valiant sub-committee were to have the Cenotaph stripped of this, which should not be difficult, they would really have one of the most effective statues in the Empire.

From what I have heard upon what seems good

authority there would be ample scope here for an active Society for the Protection of Natives from Cruelty, especially in cases of labour in outlying farms. No doubt there are British brutes as well as Dutch brutes, it so happens that the cases which have been brought to my notice are Dutch, and the Dutch have the name of being more harsh with the natives than the British. What is needed is that when cases arise there should be someone who will see that the injured or dead native gets fair play, and that the criminal is really punished. This is not so at present, and there have been recent cases of murder when the condemned have got off with trivial fines. If a strong representative of a Society were present, it would stiffen up the bench.

In the Roos case two Boers were arraigned for beating a Kaffir boy to death and then hiding his body in an antheap in the hope that the insects would destroy it. The boy's brother, who had also been beaten, escaped and gave information. The facts were obvious, but the men escaped with a fine. Several similar cases were brought to my notice. The bulk of the Dutch are just as kind-hearted as the British, but it is these occasional savages who do such deeds and who should be severely dealt with. Apart from the moral aspect, there is a great political danger in the general disaffection caused by such cases among the natives. But the moral responsibility is the chief thing. Better that Great Britain had no connection with South

Africa than that she should be tainted with the torture and murder of helpless natives. I am sure, however, that a single case of severe punishment would set matters right, and a strong S.P.C.N. would be the agent to bring this about.

After writing this paragraph a good deal more evidence was laid before me as to the ill-treatment of natives in country parts and the failure of magistrates to do their duty. In two cases in the same district within the last eighteen months two natives had been shot by farmers, one killed and the other maimed, but in both cases the culprits were acquitted on the excuse that they thought they had fired at game. At Rustenburg a Kaffir boy was beaten to death. The magistrate gave six months as a penalty. This magistrate's name was, I believe, British, so my indictment is not racial though the culprits in each case were Dutch. In yet another case a manager shot a Kaffir boy dead, and was acquitted. Now I see a case reported in the morning paper which runs as follows:

BETHAL, *Tuesday.*
"Two Europeans, J. Nafte (38), an unmarried farmer, of Bankpan, and his foreman, J.J. van Niekerk, married, aged about 28, are now in custody as the sequel to the death of a native on their farm yesterday. It is alleged, on account of some misbehaviour, the deceased native was seized yesterday morning and tied up to a wagon with a reim round his neck, and kept in this position for two hours. It is further alleged

that, after he had been released, the native was taken into the kitchen. There were no eye-witnesses as to what occurred in the kitchen, but a noise was heard by bystanders, and it is stated that the native was seen to crawl out on all fours later on. Further allegations are that the native was later hung up on a tree by one leg and then struck several blows. The native died at about 3 p.m. Yesterday afternoon the police at Bethal were informed by the foreman, J.J. van Niekerk, that there was a dead native outside their kitchen door. He is alleged to have stated to the police that he had no knowledge how the deceased got there, or what had happened to him. He also informed the police that all the other boys were missing from the farm. At eight o'clock last night all the remaining boys, 72 in number, came up to the police station. As the result, the police made investigations. The District Surgeon made a post-mortem examination on the deceased, which disclosed the following injuries: The back was beaten to a jelly; there were three ribs broken, the breast-bone was cracked, and there were several other bruises all over the body. Jack Nafte and Johannes Jacobus van Niekerk were arrested this evening on a charge of murder, and were lodged in the local jail."[1]

Do I exaggerate then if I say that there should be an inquiry and some steps taken if such things are done under what is still nominally the British flag? At the same time it is only fair to quote what is Mrs. Millin's final comment upon this question. She says:

"The Boer's attitude towards the native is benignity itself compared with the Belgian's in the Congo, the German's in South-West Africa, the Portuguese on the

---

[1] The upshot of this case was a trivial sentence for one man and seven years for the other.

East Coast. And at least there are never in South Africa, as in America, burnings and lynchings of black men.

"But," she adds, "in the end, except for the English ideal, for the Cape tradition, for the passionate service of here and there a hot-hearted South African, the Kaffir has little hope of generous treatment in the midst of white people."

In connection with the subject of native ill-treatment, a prominent resident in the Free State has pointed out that such crimes are very rare there, though they are common in the Transvaal. "There is one recent case," he writes, "of a native girl being tied to the back of a cart and made to run miles. She was then tied to a wagon in a shed and was found dead soon afterwards. I think the brute was fined 10s., but I am not sure of this. Anyhow, I am certain that the fine was not more than £2." This case inspired a fine poem which went the round of the South African Press and ended with the verse:

> "Ours is the fall, not yours; this will reflect
>   Upon the very future of us all,
> Honour, prestige and justice and respect,
>   So much of this is lost, so far we fall."

Another man of British birth, who had lived long in the backveld and had served five years in the police, gave me a considered report in which he said that in spite of occasional bad cases the general treatment of the native by the Boer was not bad, and that in some ways it was better than that which is given by the Britisher. His point was that the British wanted things done in an orderly way and kept the native at arm's length while giving him cold justice. On the other hand, the Boer would yarn with him by the hour, had a close community of interests, and was altogether much more personal and intimate. For this reason, he said, a Boer can get his farm labour cheaper than an Englishman can do. On the other hand, while making this defence of the Boer, this man writes: "No native has a hope against a Boer with a backveld jury. Any British juryman put in the box is challenged as a matter of routine. In a recent case a farmer chased a Kaffir into the veld with his car, ran over him, and drove off, leaving him with a broken leg. All the British jurymen were challenged and the Boer jury found 'not guilty', to the indignation of the judge. Outside one juryman admitted that they all knew the accused had done it but if they found guilty it would give the Kaffir a civil case for perhaps £500, and a Kaffir is not worth it."

This same correspondent, who is, as has been shown, by no means hostile to the Boers and pleads their case as against the British employer, is very dark as to the racial situation. He says: "It amounts to this, that the young Africander ever since '02 and increasingly of later years has been bred up in an atmosphere of anti-English feeling, fed up on Hobhouse lies and 'liberal' slanders about the Boer War. I have myself been told by educated men that no German atrocities in Belgium were a patch on the horrors perpetrated by us in 1899–1902. To-day," he continues, "the decent old-style Botha type of Boer hardly dares to be seen chatting with an English friend in the village street. To be heard speaking English is to be suspect." All this is very depressing, but I am bound from reports coming from all sides to conclude that the division between the races is still a deep one and that it may in the future lead to some sad catastrophe.

Last night I was a proud father. The meeting was an excellent one. There was not a vacant seat in the theatre, and the Mayor presided. When question time came I was asked whether other members of the family had psychic experiences as well as myself. I replied that some of them had their own separate experiences apart from me, and that my son, who was now on the platform, would perhaps consent to tell them one. Denis, who was not entirely unprepared for such an ordeal, rose at once, advanced to the table, and in a quiet but very audible voice and with dignity of manner, gave the audience the story of the return of his friend, the Hon. David Duncombe. It was admirably done, and considering that he had never spoken from any platform in his life, it was a wonderful example of cool courage. The audience listened entranced to the story.

The bald facts were these. This young man, who was the heir to the earldom of Feversham, was killed by a lorry when driving at night on the Great North Road. He belonged to a little coterie who called themselves "the gang", all close friends and devoted to motor-racing. Both my boys were members of it. Denis was a very close friend, so after the young fellow's death he went to consult Mrs. Barkel, making the appointment anonymously at the Psychic College. The medium sank into trance and his friend took possession of her. He was overjoyed to come, said that he was happy, sent messages by name to each of the gang, gave their nicknames, and alluded in a chaffing way to their personal habits, discussed with the knowledge of an expert a new racing car which my boys had bought, alluded to a physical weakness which he had in life but which was so concealed that none save Denis knew of it, and finally drew a plan of how the accident occurred, showing that his own driving, of which he was proud, was in nowise to blame. As Denis said, "for an hour my friend might himself have been sitting in the chair in front of me." I do not think there could have been one person in the audience who did not know in his bones that every word my son said was true. But if so, do I exaggerate when I say that it is the greatest advance in knowledge which has ever come to mankind?

On the day following this incident Denis had another remarkable experience. It seems that there is a certain witch doctor or prophetess near the borders of Zululand who said to the Commissioner of those parts that her Spirits had given her a special message which she was to deliver to the white man who would come speaking about Spirits in Durban. This was told me when I arrived, but as I had only one clear day and was a tired man I did not feel that I should spend it on a journey of over a hundred miles on country roads. Denis, however, volunteered to go, and the Ashton Jonsons went with them. They came back greatly impressed. The woman lived in a real native kraal at the back of beyond. She was youngish, intelligent, with her face covered with yellow ochre and weird adornments, such as snakes' bladders in her hair. She fell into trance, which was assisted by the moanings and cries of several other women, just as we use music for vibrations upon some physic occasions. The first communications, which were translated sentence by sentence, purported to come from some dead warrior who expressed pleasure at seeing whites and blacks meeting in friendship at the black man's home. Then the seeress led my son away, saying that his message was for me alone. "Tell the Mulungu" (this epithet means "a white stranger") "that his mission here is a great one and will have success. Tell him that great opposition was prepared to make it fail, but that this opposition had been beaten and was now crumbling. Tell him that he and his family will go back safely across the great waters to his own land." That was the general purport of the message, which is in no way evidential and yet is cheering none the less. What could this obscure Zulu woman, who speaks no English, know normally about me or my message? Denis photographed the lady, and was, as I understand, followed by all the maidens of the kraal until he found shelter in the motor.

We leave Durban with real regret. We all thought that it was the jolliest town which we had met in all our travels. The reason for this is that the most magnificent bathing beach in the world is within five minutes' tram ride from the centre of the town, with glorious white-capped breakers rolling in from the Indian Ocean. One could not wish to see a more exhilarating sight than all the hundreds of bright-coloured bathing dresses flashing in and out from among the high creaming rollers. It is a great playmate, the sea, and a rough romp with it is Nature's finest sport; but always it is like the tiger cub, which is so kittenish and velvety, and so delightful to play with, until some day it stretches out a lazy paw and tears its playmate's shoulder off. So one plays long with the sea, and then some fine day there is a waving of white arms and a convulsed face, and one more victim goes out with the undertow.

It is a capricious playmate – and there perhaps lies its charm.

One cannot discuss Natal without some allusion to the East Indian problem, which is certainly a most vexatious and difficult one. About 1860 the sugar-growers, dissatisfied with Kaffir labour, asked leave to import coolies from India. The experiment was only too successful. After the odious caste regulations of India the poorer Hindoos found the unrestricted freedom of Natal to be a heavenly condition, and the matter grew to such alarming proportions that vessels full of Indians had at last to be warned off from Durban. By that time, however, the mischief was done. The men who had served their indentures in the sugar-fields had settled down, and by their thrift and industry were filling up all such positions as waiters, artisans, small traders and so forth, in such a way that the white man, already heavily handicapped by Kaffir menial labour, had hardly any sure ground of his own. Such is still the position. At the present moment there are just about as many Asiatics as there are Europeans in Natal, and, useful as they are, it is their very virtues which make them dangerous to the white Africans who have to fight hard for existence. It is all very well for the Imperialist to say that a member of the Empire must have the free run of every country in the Empire but in actual practice the question is the most difficult of all the difficult questions which this distracted land has to solve.

In the other States of the Union the Indian question

took a less acute form, as they had not been actually invited to come in, as in Natal. None the less there has been a great deal of friction, and finally an Indian agent-general has been appointed to represent the interests of these people. The late agent, whose term has only just expired, Mr. Sastri, left a very high reputation as a thinker and an orator. It was in the earlier stages of this contention that the famous Ghandi, who had come over as a highly educated barrister to conduct a case, and who found himself treated as a Kaffir, made his mark as a politician by the fine way in which he upheld the rights of his countrymen. Personally I felt nothing but sympathy for these gentle, quiet, and very efficient people.

To-day, December 13th, we leave for Johannesburg, which is from a lecturing point of view the culminating point of our journey. Up to now it has been an unbroken success. We approach the last stage with a high heart.

CHAPTER V

The Eastern Transvaal – South African Problems – The Native Strike – The Mean White – The Learned and the Humble – The Rustenburg Spirit Photograph – Pretoria – Professor Kovaloff – A Warning to Investors.

As you wake in the early morning and get your first glimpse of the South-Eastern Transvaal in the Standerton district, you feel at this time of year that you have never seen such a picture of pastoral perfection. The veld is there, but the kopjes are gone, or are only represented by occasional low hillocks. So far as the eyes can reach, in every direction there stretches the one unbroken green plain with countless flocks and herds upon it. The farms would seem to be very large, for it is only at long intervals that a farmhouse is visible.

Then after some hours of travel the monotony of the plain is broken by a strange object. At first I could make nothing of it. It was an enormous snow-white pile, a small hill, with the sun gleaming brightly upon it. Had we then come into a chalk country? No, there were none of those gracious gentle curves which make the chalk downs so satisfying. Besides this huge white mound was glimmering in the light. Then suddenly I realized. This was the white sand and powdered quartz which formed the spoil heap of a gold-mine, and we had come upon an outlying shaft of the great Rand reef – the greatest treasure-house in the world, from which, up to date, 1,000 million pounds worth of gold have been extracted at a steady rate of 40 million a year. I wonder if it is generally realized in England that the South African gold output is rather more than half the total output of the world. One wonders what would have become of our currency, and how it could have kept pace with the increased demands upon it, if this huge addition had not been made.

One wonders too – the world is full of wonderments, and when you cease to appreciate the fact your brain is ceasing to function – one wonders how on earth this river of gold-bearing conglomerate, which has now been traced to a length of 60 miles and to the breadth of 3 miles and to the depth of more than a mile, ever came to be there. Geology is vague upon the matter. It is on the watershed, the ridge, dividing the slopes which lead down to two considerable rivers, the Vaal and the Limpopo. That may have some remote bearing upon the subject. There is granite below, the usual old skeleton of the earth. Then comes sand and clay in the usual alternate layers, and interleaved with this is the queer "banket" formation, which consists of water-worn pebbles in a kind of cement or conglomerate, this cement being full of gold and iron. After this strange formation had been laid down, thick forests, which left their traces in coal-beds, formed on the top – the said coal-beds being denuded for the most part, but still existing and actually penetrated by the mine shafts at the east end of the ridge. So now the reader knows as much as I do about the matter.

But there is yet another point of rather tragic interest. Half the available gold has in forty years been extracted. If the costs of working rise, as they continually do, then much of the remainder may never be got. But at the best one could not reckon upon more than forty years. And then what becomes of this great city in which I now sit, and where I have to close the windows and sit in the heat in order to keep out the incessant roar and hoot of the traffic? "There where the long street roared is now the silence of the central sea." So it may soon be. But a deserted city exposed to the heavens 6,000 feet high in the air under the glare of an African sun would be a more dreadful sight than a submerged one. However, "Sufficient for the day . . ." Johannesburg goes on its way care-free. It is light-hearted and full of vitality. After all, as Shaw has profoundly remarked, "you never can tell." Who would have foretold that platinum would suddenly appear as an addition to the huge mineral wealth of South Africa? But the trouble is that new developments can hardly take place exactly here, and population will follow the course of these discoveries.

One by one the old mines are gutted and abandoned, so that the only hope lies in opening up new ones. Even as I write the famous Ferreira Deep has reached its last clean up. Its life has been thirty years, and during that time 130 tons of pure gold have been won from it. Nearly half of this was profit, and the dividends have totalled 700 per cent. No wonder that the men who came early, the Barnatos and Robinsons, became among the richest of mankind.

I don't think the average man in England has the least idea of the huge scale of all this business. Here is one small pointer which, may give an idea of it. Some years ago a strike was called (an unheard-of thing) among the black workers on the mines. Some of them were called up. How many do you suppose emerged? Seventy thousand – no less. Imagine every shaft and outlet spouting up these black devils from the depths of the earth. It was like a scene in one of Wells' phantasies. The general feeling was one of horror and of "For God's sake get them out of sight on any terms." At present the average wage is £3 a month, as compared with about £1 a month which a Kaffir can get in agriculture. But every time there is a rise in the mine wages it puts some big block of ore matter outside the margin of profitable working, so that there is not much room for generosity. That is the terrible thing about all these wage questions, whether at home or abroad. A union forces the employer to pay a high wage. The employer economizes by using fewer hands, or possibly is driven out of business altogether. The result is that other workmen are left entirely unemployed. You have a sheltered trade, like the railwaymen, who have good wages. Instantly the coal trade suffers from higher railway charges and the weight falls on the miners. Who would not wish to give every man of every trade enough to live in decent comfort? And yet the cold fact remains that the real choice lies between some having more while others have less, or many having something intermediate. Every workman who is artificially overpaid causes some other workman to have less than his due.

There are some dark shadows on this glittering, bustling city of gold. One is the possible exhaustion of the reef. A second lies with that huge black contingent down in the depths. A third is organized white labour, which is restless and occasionally turbulent, in spite of its pound a day. These are all three only a menace which may never in our generation come to a serious head. But there is a fourth which is always present. It depends upon the presence of very large numbers of poor whites, men for whom it is impossible to find humble work, since the Kaffir does it both cheaper and better. They are very numerous, these men – indeed, it has been calculated that one out of ten of the total white population of South Africa come under this heading. What is one to do with them? They are not only unemployed, but have often become unemployable. They are desperate men, with nothing to hope for, nothing to live for, ready to take advantage of any strife or turmoil, since no change can ever make them worse. It was they who turned the strike of 1922 into something very near a revolution, when the insurgents were only put down after desperate fighting. Moscow may have brought the match, but the powder was already there – and is still there. The mean white question is one of several which South Africa has to solve. What is the use of immigration when all these men are waiting hopelessly for a job? It seems an extreme measure to export men out of a young country, but I really think the logical thing would be to send 50,000 of these men to some part of Australia which could absorb them. At present the Government attempts from time to time to placate them by putting them on to various public works and constructions, with the result that the said work is badly done and enormously expensive. I saw, for example, some figures comparing the cost of the great Australian dam (Buranjack, I think, is the name, but I have no book of reference) and the Hartebeeste dam near Pretoria. The Australian dam is many times larger and more effective, but cost nearly a million pounds less. This, according to my informant, was due to the attempt of the Government to give work to the poor whites.

This monstrous digression represents some of the general views which came to me during my stay in the city – superficial no doubt, but at least unprejudiced. Now let me descend to our personal experiences.

There are two outstanding hotels in the town – the Langham, which is quiet but rather out of the way, and the Carlton, which cannot help being noisy, as it is at the junction of the two main streets, Eloff and Commissioner, but is in its construction up-to-date, though the details leave much to be desired. Here we established ourselves, and as we only got in on the Friday and my first lecture was on the Sunday I had to keep quiet and try to acclimatize, for it is no joke to ascend 6,000 feet and then speak for two hours in a large hall.

None the less, the lecture went very well and I had an enormous audience. There was a certain atmosphere of criticism, which is not unwelcome to me, so long as it is expressed, in a courteous fashion. I was conscious of it at the beginning, but I felt that it had worn very thin before the end. One man had expressed his disapprobation by grunts of dissent, and drew up some damaging question in writing, but had so little sympathy from his neighbours that none of them would help to pass it up, and he had to return it to his pocket. It was a most successful evening, and the photographic lecture, three days later, was equally so. The theatre was too small, however, and very many were turned away. We heard of one couple who had journeyed 500 miles, or 1,000 altogether, to be present. Fortunately they got seats. I met these people afterwards and found that though they lived at the back of the Limpopo River they had an excellent psychic library and were quite up-to-date in every respect. When I considered their knowledge of these all-important matters, and compared it with the comparative ignorance of some of the best brains in London, the Keiths, the Inges, and the Barnes, it made me appreciate that old passage about things being withheld from the wise and learned while they were granted to the humble.

I am surprised to find how widespread the knowledge is here. Apart from the organized Spiritualist Churches, which are several, there is a great amount of private inquiry and appreciation. Yesterday (December 21st) we were invited to a very select party at the Country Club, and found that among thirty guests, who were all respected citizens of the town, there was not one who was not a well-informed psychic student. This Country Club is a perfectly beautiful place on the edge of the town, provided with swimming baths and every possible luxury. As there is a second club, the Automobile, which is equally luxurious, the town is well provided with the amenities of life. When I think, however, of the toiling, invisible thousands underground, it is rather like the opening scenes of that wonderful German film, which shows the robot and the superman. *Absit omen!* On that very evening a splendid young man wrung me by the hand because he thought that I had done something to keep him from suicide, to which he was driven by poverty and unemployment. It is indeed a strange and a pitiable world.

I get many alleged psychic photographs submitted to me in the course of my travels, most of which I am compelled to turn down. I have no doubt many of them are genuine, but I cannot afford to take risks and I accept nothing which does not seem to me to bear absolute proof. I have just had one sent to me by post which really does seem to be true, and the *Star* newspaper having learned of it published it with the note from me: "I have examined the photograph and, accepting Mrs. McKerrill's account as correct, I have no doubt that the face in the tree is beyond chance and is therefore psychic."

It is now known as the Rustenburg photograph and has naturally produced some sensation in the town. To-day there is a long interview with the husband in the papers. He roundly declares that he is an atheist, so cannot be suspected of spiritualistic sympathies. But he is completely dumbfounded, because the face, he declares, is the image of Keir Hardie, with whom he was very intimate as a younger man. It is certainly a curious case, for, granting that it is psychic, who is the medium, and if the medium is the husband or the wife, why do they not get other results? She is an unskilled photographer, the film is one of six in a Kodak roll, and it was developed by some chemist in the town. Altogether it is worthy of a place in my collection.

To-day (December 23rd) I lectured at Pretoria, which necessitated a very long day. The capital is 35 miles from Johannesburg, and through the kindness of Mr. Hunt we were provided with two cars which carried our whole party across. The road is an excellent one. I found the town much enlarged, and we agreed that on the whole we should give it the palm as being the most beautiful inland town we have seen. Our vote is worth something, for we have seen many cities. Perhaps Salt Lake City would beat it – but few others. Pretoria lies in a beautiful amphitheatre of hills, it is framed in delicate greens, is itself well wooded, and is brightly coloured and very free from smoke. The public buildings were remarkably fine even in 1900, but now the central square is really superb, and so too is the new federal house of parliament, for it may be news to the English reader that the Government of the South African Union oscillates between Cape Town and Pretoria according to the season, so that duplicates have to be found of everything. A member of parliament gets £700 a year, but he must have many inconveniences to make up.

In the afternoon the courteous host of the Grand Hotel drove us round all the beauty spots, including the fine Country Club, giving us the chance of inspecting one of the old forts which were bogies to us before the Boer War. It seemed to me a perfect death-trap, pathetically inadequate. There are, of course, no guns mounted, and it is simply a show place now. It was never fit to be anything else.

They have erected in front of the station the Kruger statue, which stood in old days in the middle of the central square. They could make nothing of the fine old fellow artistically. His one request to the sculptor was that he should be done in his top-hat, and that the top-hat be hollow like a saucer so that the birds could find water there. But in spite of the homely central figure the four statues of kneeling Boers which flank each corner are really magnificent. Their four splendidly rugged heads, so full of character, seem to reflect the whole history of the country. It reminded me of the remarkable Canadian monument in Montreal, where at each corner there is a voyageur, an Indian, and so forth. They seem really national, such monuments as that. How is it that in London we have no such memorials, inspired by the true historical sense tinged with romance? Look at the row of Guardsmen on the Horse Guards parade to show how unimaginative we are. I can only recall two statues in London – Boadicea on Westminster Bridge, and the artillery monument at Hyde Park Corner – as the ones which have ever given me a thrill, though Lawes' Chariot on the gate into St. James's Park is certainly finely decorative in effect. The Briton, the Saxon, the Dane and the Norman would surely make four fine corners of a pedestal.

My audience in the evening was appreciative and select, but less numerous than usual. The town is half Dutch, and the Dutch Reformed Church is, as the Du Plessis case showed, a shut box incapable of holding anything that is new. The ruin will slowly crumble away, but it takes time and continued assaults of truth. The lecture had to be at nine, it was nearly eleven before I concluded, so after a delightful drive with the fivefold jewel of the Southern Cross hanging before us against a deep violet curtain, we reached our Carlton Hotel at one in the morning – a fairly full day.

At Pretoria again I found the Jewish Rabbi, a very cultivated man, to be an interested member of my audience, while the Christian Churches hung aloof. I had a chat with him afterwards, and found that he appreciated the truth and the breadth of our teaching. However, I find that some of our orthodox friends have yielded to reason. I had a letter to-day from the daughter of an eminent Churchman, the Rev. A.V. Magee, who had many scraps with me in the Press in days gone by. She says: "He opposed you strongly because he thought it was against the teaching of the Church. He became, however, completely converted, and just before his death in 1923 he told my brother and me how wrong he felt he had been and how one should strive to keep in touch with the spirit world."

I have met recently an interesting personality, Professor Kovaloff, who was once Minister of Mines in Russia. When he was driven out he was easily able to find a place for himself in the world, for he is recognized as one of the great authorities upon platinum, and the future of platinum with its allied minerals, palladium and the rest, is the most pressing of all mining questions here, since large deposits have been found in the Northern Transvaal. I understand that the platinum beds in the Urals are very much more extensive than the South African, and that Russia can turn the metal out much more cheaply than is done here, so unless some agreement is made restricting output, as in the case of diamonds, and such agreement is international, the price can hardly be sustained. The present price of platinum here is £15 per ounce, which certainly does seem fictitious if the deposits are large and extraction easy. Kovaloff is a good Spiritualist who has a real grasp of the subject, which is rare, and agrees with me that it is destined to cause a revolution in human thought and to destroy that materialism which has been the cause of all our misfortunes and will entirely destroy us unless we can find the antidote.

Talking of diamonds, the situation is really becoming grotesque. One who was in a position to know tells me that they are literally shovelling them out now in Namaqualand, the gravel there being full of them. They are withheld from the market, but of course these huge accumulations are not destroyed, and there must be a horde somewhere – it would be indiscreet to say where – which would give a thrill to every Raffles in the world. But in the meantime what a network of adventurers, and police, and illicit buyers must exist, and what an enormous right of search and interference with liberty must be involved! There is also great danger of political corruption, since alterations in the law make all the difference to the rich companies, and the law is, as a matter of fact, continually tilted in their direction. No doubt Solly Joel, Oppenheim, and the others who are at the heart of the matter, are perfectly honourable men, but the situation is, I think, both difficult and dangerous. It may become impossible as fresh deposits are found in different parts of the world.

Another man of note whom I met is Mr. Shepperd, once militant governor of the town in the old war. He very gracefully gave Billy a fine emerald, saying,

"Remember that this was given you by an old Boer who would gladly have shot your father thirty years ago." It was a charming episode.

In a previous portion of this rambling narrative I spoke of the good prospects of the man who comes out here with a couple of thousand pounds, some knowledge of farming, a stout heart and a pair of willing hands. "If they make up their minds to rough it and do not expect to get rich quick, or make fortunes, they will have a fine, healthy, useful life. As for droughts and plagues, the whole of the country shows farmers who have weathered these handicaps and are now established. What they have done others can do." So writes Leonard Flemming. But a caution is needed here. What he talks of are large 1,000-acre farms run by men of experience. It by no means applies to those small orange or citrus plantations which have absorbed much good British money and given little or no return. Some years ago there was an outbreak of advertisements in the home Press which gave the idea that if a man bought a small fruit-growing plantation of this sort it would yield him a steady income, even if he himself were not there in person. The idea of the absentee fruit-grower could only have appealed to most ignorant people, for surely it is common knowledge that one does not simply pick an orange off a tree and sell it to someone who is leaning over the fence, but that sorting, grading, packing and marketing are a science in itself. The result has been disastrous, and the only good to be got from it now is to make it serve as a warning. There was the Zebedelia Estates, in which nearly 1,000 people, many of them naval and military officers, bought five-acre plots at from, £500 to £700 per plot. No one, after eight years, has had any return. The same applies to "Prudential Estates," "East Rand Orchards" and other such concerns. It has all been dead loss falling upon a class which has very limited capital. Not more than 2 per cent of the investors came out to live on their plots, which perhaps may be as well since at the best the scheme had little chance. An agency has been formed by Sir Herbert Matthews at 28 Westminster Palace Gardens. S.W., to do what can be done for these poor people, and this short note may serve to put some of them in touch with it.

CHAPTER VI

South African Art – The Coming of the Fairies – Teetotal
Revelry – General Tanner – Louis Botha's Letters – The Flag
– The Robinson Mine – The Slums – The Native Bazaar –
Bishop Karney – Our Sunday Service – The Premier Diamond
Mine – The Future of Johannesburg.

I try, so far as I can, when I am in any country to sample
the literature, art and drama of that country, so as to get
something of the soul of the people. One does not find
much to work upon in South Africa. Oliver Schreiner's
little masterpiece is the one abiding monument of the
past. In art I saw some passable South African landscapes
and some fine sculpture, but I had few opportunities. In
the drama I was amused by Stephen Black's *Backveld
Boer*, an amusing piece, where the primitive farmer
scores in approved fashion over the degenerate English
family into which he is precipitated. The "Voortrekkers"
cinema may be put down as South African art, and it is
most excellent. In literature they have Leonard
Flemming, whom I have already quoted, and who is no
mean poet on occasion. C.R. Prance, author of *Island
Sea Lions*, is a writer who deserves a far wider audience

than he has found. Mrs. Millin is also a writer of great distinction, and her *South Africans* is the best book upon the country that I have seen. She is, I understand, a Jewess. Mr. William Westrup, who has written some excellent novels, is, I believe, a native of Durban. These are a few with whom I have come in touch, and if I did better in Australia, perhaps the fault is my own.

The constant noise of the city has got rather on our nerves. Our rooms are at the corner of two main streets, and a horrible belching, screaming, gobbling, grunting and coughing of cars goes on for eighteen hours on end. There is a good deal of unrestrained selfishness in the unnecessary uproar which the cars make – especially in the early morning. I wonder what old Carlyle, who objected to the cackle of a few hens, would make of this pandemonium! We have found, however, a partial cure in the delightful Country Club, one of the most charming gardens in the world, which lies on the edge of the city. Thither we go now in the morning, and there we stay, taking books and necessaries with us, under the shade of glorious trees, watching the flowers and the butterflies, until work calls us back. It is a most blessed respite.

My third lecture at Johannesburg was on the night of Sunday, December 30th. It consisted chiefly of ordinary psychic photographs, but in honour of the festive season I added to it the fairy photographs which seemed to please the people immensely. It is amazing how difficult it is to eradicate a lie. I find that there are thousands of people who still believe the wild assertion made years ago that the fairy photographs were taken from a well-known advertisement. I took the line in my lecture that I was prepared to consider any explanation of these results, save only one which attacked the character of the children. I am sure that when I had explained the facts there were few in the Hall who were not prepared to accept the photographs. I showed also the Devonshire tree spirit and the new German fairy photographs. My book analysing the evidence about the fairies is the first serious treatment of what may prove to be a new order of life upon this planet since a book in the Middle Ages which was called, if I remember right, *The Secret Commonwealth* (an excellent title!). There have been many objections made to the Cottingley photographs, most of them palpably absurd. The one which merits most attention is that they are cleverly cut-out figures which have been held up by invisible threads. Such an explanation is conceivable, but the balance of proba-bility seems to me to be greatly against it. The reasons for rejecting such a solution are as follows:

1. Frances, the younger girl, wrote at the time (1917) that Cottingley was a nice place on account of the but-terflies and fairies. This card was sent to her friend in South Africa (who came from South Africa) and was unearthed in 1923, or thereabouts, and published in the

Cape Argus. For what possible reason would she, a child of ten, write thus, if she knew it was a deception?

2. If the figures were cut out, then similar figures must be in existence in other copies of the book or paper. These have not been found.

3. There is a great difference in solidity between the 1920 figures and those of 1917, which could be accounted for by waning mediumship, but which is inconsistent with faking.

4. Experts have reported signs of movement in the figures.

5. Mr. Gardner formed a high opinion of the character both of the children and of their father. The latter would certainly have known if there were deception.

All these reasons make a case which, if it is not to my mind absolutely final, like the case for psychic phenomena, is at least a very strong one. But many fresh corroborations are needed before the fairies take their recognized place in Nature.

Can one invent any kind of plausible explanation which would fit the fairies, into the general scheme of Nature? I can only think of one, which is, I admit, grotesque and fantastic, but not beyond the limits of what is possible. We may have underrated the capacity for adaptation of any species when it is hard pressed for existence. Fish should not fly in the ordinary course of Nature, and yet we know that a species of fish has learned to fly in order to preserve itself. Now, let us suppose that in very early days, the days when insects predominated in the world, some insect species which was hard pressed found that by some change of vibration it could become invisible to its, enemies. We see such a phenomenon every time the fans of the electric punkah begin to revolve. They vanish. We will suppose these creatures learned to vanish. After a time they would develop a life and an evolution of their own upon this new vibration unseen to the human eye. Having in their new medium powers of creation and imitation such as we do not possess, they could imitate the human body more or less perfectly without having attained the human soul or spirit – always retaining some trace of their insect origin. Far-fetched – but possible. Imagination is the irresponsible scout who rides in advance of the solid phalanx of Science.

The final lecture was memorable to me as Denis took the chair, and carried it off most excellently. At the end I thanked the Johannesburg audiences for their unvarying courtesy to me, and added that I wished to thank the Press for the fair play and kindliness they had shown. Now my work here is done save for the religious service next week. For this we have taken the Orpheum, which holds 2,000 people, and I have sent for Mrs. Kimpton of Maritzburg, who did so well with her clairvoyance at Cape Town. We hope to have a great evening, and to get at the poorer people, since there is no charge for admission. If I could travel for nothing with my party and be housed for nothing, I would never wish to charge at all.

Last night New Year was seen in at that earthly paradise, the Country Club. We danced until the crowd became so thick that there was hardly room to rotate. Finally we elders came away before midnight and left the youngsters to carry on. Malcolm nearly became involved in a fight, as he heard someone abusing me over Spiritualism, and instantly took the matter up in his own fiery way. The fellow was three-quarters drunk, but he had sense enough to realize that he had met heavier metal than himself, and he climbed down. Denis got back at 8.30 in the morning after a night's adventures with a chosen party, "beating them up" as they phrase it. And all this on tea! The young generation is wonderful!

Well, here we are in 1929! What will it bring? It made me solemn to see the giddy throng last night, men and women so light-hearted, and to reflect upon the chances of the future. When one is elderly one has no personal fears, but Fate, like some savages, may hit you through those you love. But we have been well guarded up to now, and our road seems to lie very straight before us. I think that perhaps I have earned a little rest and may be able to do more work without incessant interruptions at home. The constant travel and speaking are very wearying.

To-day, New Year's day, we enjoyed the hospitality of Dr. Erasmus Ellis and his charming wife. Dr. Ellis is one of the leading physicians, and I can speak with knowledge of his powers, for I am a grateful patient. At his table we met General Tanner, the gallant leader of the South African Brigade in the War, and we had much interesting talk. There was a French officer there also who gave sidelights upon the subject, and a fine clergyman who had fought all through with the carnal weapon as a captain in the Leicestershires. We all agreed that if General French had pulled out of the battle line early in September, 1914, as he was within an ace of doing, it would have been an indelible disgrace to the British arms. I cannot imagine how so brave and honourable a man could have conceived of such an action.

General Tanner told me that he had seen the correspondence of Louis Botha when he was leading the Boers against us, and that he had several times said in his letters that the Boer resistance could not continue unless the British would take charge of the Boer women and children, which he had repeatedly asked them to do. This bears very directly upon that monument at Bloemfontein – or rather not upon the monument but upon the bitter inscription, for we can all agree that the poor women and children should have their memorial.

I am more and more impressed by the extreme tension among the British population here. They are deeply dissatisfied with existing conditions. "It is very nearly as bad as the Kruger regime," said one of the leaders of Johannesburg Society to-day. "If a situation is vacant, an Englishman has not a dog's chance of getting it," said another. "My people have been in this country for four generations, since 1820," said another, "and I am made to feel that I am a foreigner." The flag question is still a sore one, and yet personally I cannot see why the two flags should not fly together, or why the descendants of the brave men who first opened up the country should not have their own symbol, if they want it, so long as ours also goes with it. I know that my view will not be acceptable to the British, but none the less I feel that it would have been better not to disfigure the South African flag by what look like three postage stamps stuck in the middle of it. It is irritating to the Dutch and does no good to the British. The two flags flying side by side seem to me to meet the case. On the other hand, this Nationalist Government by its commercial treaty with Germany, which deliberately breaks the ring of Imperial preference, has caused justifiable indignation. I think also that the British have a real grievance in the language question. Every civil servant of every sort has to know Afrikaans as well as English. All the Dutch – or all the educated Dutch – know English as a matter of course, so that the law involves no hardship, but it is a very great hardship that every Englishman who wishes to share the public life of the country should have to learn what is really a barbarous dialect without roots or literature. I have wondered whether a deal might not be made with the Nationalists, and the postage stamps taken off the flag if they in turn will make the language clause apply only to all-Dutch districts. Until the double grievance is removed there will be no peace in South Africa.

We spent the morning of January 4th doing the Robinson mine. We did not descend, for the workings are now at a depth of 6,000 feet, and it is no small task to go down to them. The increased depth means higher expenses in working, and the ore does not improve as it descends, so that there seems to be a point at which operations may become difficult. This part of the reef has been long worked. If one wishes to make an investment now, it is rather to the east end of the reef, which is both newer and richer, that one must go.

We saw the whole process from the moment when the great chunks of grey rock, with no indication of gold in them, and looking like ordinary road metal, came to the surface, until it was broken and chewed and pulverized, amidst horrible stampings and uproar, flowing out at last as a sort of pea-soup-coloured fluid, which carries within it 95 per cent of the total. This in turn is treated with cyanides and with heat, until at last the wonderful alchemy is accomplished, and the grey stone has utterly vanished, while a little button of yellow metal lies at the bottom of a pipkin. These in turn were, fused together until we saw an ingot worth £3,000, which with all my muscular strength I could hardly raise with one hand from the ground.

There are some terrible disease fiends which haunt the getting of gold. The first is silicitis, which means the petrifaction of the lungs from the infiltration of fine powder of flint. No inoculation can stop this, and it leads to a lingering death of terrible agony. Then there is the cyanide rash – a hideous disfigurement. Then there is mercurial poisoning, and finally the total deafness which follows upon work in the roaring stamp room. When to this is added the frequent accidents, overwinding, fall of rock, and so on, it makes a hard life. The pay, however, is good. Most of the white men have over £1 a day, while the natives get three times what they would earn on a farm. I asked the manager how the ancients managed who had no cyanide or other machinery, but his answer was that the old diggings were often alluvial, when the process is simple and primitive methods of bowl and rocker will suffice.

To-day (January 5th) I went out with the kind assent of Colonel Godley, Chief of Police, and investigated some of the more criminal of the slums of this great city. There are certainly some strange places. We were assured (Denis was with me) that if we had come into some of them alone, without police protection, we should have had a knife in our backs very quickly. When Denis wandered away he was very sternly called back. Colonel Quirk and Chief Constable Boy, who took us round, assured us that after dark they were not very healthy places even for the police, and that they always went armed.

Both of the police officials seemed to me to be very efficient men, clear-headed and practical, with a knowledge of native ways and dialects which stood them in good stead. The main object of our quest was to expose native beer supplies. These were buried in tins in the ground, and the black constables with extraordinary skill went about tapping with a stick and exposing can after can buried about a foot deep. The contents were spilled out, or were ruined by putting earth into the cans. I suppose we uncovered thirty or forty. It was foul stuff, all bubbles and nastiness, with a sickening acid smell. Some is more or less mild, but some varieties, which have carbide added to give them a kick, madden the natives, who fight wildly among themselves after drinking it. No one will admit having buried it, and the yard is common property, so you cannot prosecute the culprits, who sit round with poker faces among the other spectators. It seemed to me that they would be ruined by having their property thus destroyed, but the police assured me that most of them were rich, with £50 or £60 in their belts. "It only takes four hours to brew, and we will hardly have turned our backs before a fresh lot will be in preparation."

The worst slums which we visited, where every man is a criminal and every woman a prostitute, were on a patch of land which is outside the municipal control. I do not know why this should be so, and no doubt it will be remedied. Whereas in the Municipal Compounds the conditions are pretty good, and a family need not pay more than £1 or so a month for fair accommodation, in this awful no-man's-land they pay 25s. a week for a single room which is a mere shack. And yet, they prefer to pay this to the vile speculator who has the land rather than pay less than a quarter for decent rooms in the Municipal Compound – the reason being that they can there pursue their illegal occupations unmolested. I hope the municipality will extend their by-laws so as to sweep away these moral and sanitary plague spots.

One thing which struck me in the native bazaar, which few white men penetrate, was that the paraphernalia of the witch doctor were openly displayed for sale, whole trays of old bones, snakes' bladders, toad skins and other inconceivably nasty truck being laid out. What the filthy black magic means, or whether it means anything, I cannot make out. I should like to study it more closely. The white police are agreed that in cases of robbery the witch doctors can occasionally, and beyond all coincidence, say where the missing article or the straying cattle may be found. Was it not Saul who consulted a wise woman in order to find the lost asses of his father? But this is no more than that "far sight" which is common among our own best London mediums, and which enabled several of them to give a clear account of what became of Captain Hinchcliffe and Miss Elsie MacKay. No snakes' bladders or other horrors are needed for that. Perhaps these things are simply to impress the credulous, and ordinary clairvoyance is their only power. Certainly that Zulu woman of whom I have written knew more than would seem to be possible by ordinary means.

Another rather pitiable feature of the bazaar was the extraordinary patience and ingenuity of coloured tailors in adding patches to trousers where it would seem that to add trousers to the patch would be more reasonable and easier. I do not know why these men should wear more than a loin-cloth. It seems an offence against nature to turn the dark, clean-cut Adonis into the poor shambling scarecrow with tattered overcoat and shabby peaked cap. It is a fact, however, that on Sundays they turn out in quite well-cut suits with white collars, coloured ties, and altogether presentable. It is these half-Europeanized natives who really present, as I am told, the dangerous problem of the future. They have some very real grievances, and there are emissaries both from Russia and from America who are ready to rub them in.

Personally I am not in favour of educating them, though they educate very easily. What is the use of educating people when there is really no room for the educated? Does it not breed discontent and thwarted ambition where there was apathy if not content before? It seems to me a cruel thing to do. On the other hand, there is a lot of social education, teaching of self-respect, of self-restraint, of rational amusement, of personal cleanliness and so on which would be all to the good. There is a young English lady working among them on these lines who seemed to me to be as near a ministering angel as one could wish to meet, Miss Dorothy Maud her name. She is the daughter of the Bishop of Kensington, and he may well be proud of her. She is not twenty, a typical high-spirited open-air English girl whom one would back at sight for a champonship at golf or tennis. Yet she spends her days working among the little black children, teaching their poor mothers how to best adapt themselves to the artificial conditions of the compounds. She is building a recreation-room for them and she has no money. Her address is Y.W.C.A., Jeppe Street, Johannesburg.

I have had a good-humoured turn-up with Bishop Karney of this city. I know him to be a good man, for I have read some writings of his which show his humanity, but like so many clericals he will go out of his way to attack Spiritualism, and yet shows in his attack how ignorant he is of the very elements of the subject. Such people read one or two books written by some bigot against us, and then imagine that they know something of the subject, which is very much as if one were to try to understand the Church of Rome by reading Mr. Kensit and nothing more. I pointed out in my letter to the Press that whereas the Bishop repeated the stale old assertion that nothing but what is trivial comes through, the case was quite the opposite, and that from the wonderful writings of Andrew Jackson Davis, a man who had no education and yet who outlined a universal philosophy, down to those of Stainton Moses, of Vale Owen, of the Cleophas Script, and even, on a smaller scale, of my own "Pheneas Speaks", we have had a remarkable series of communications which bear every mark of high inspiration. One must remember also that what is trivial to the cold observer may by no means be so to the person intimately concerned, who gets his vital evidence from small matters of detail. If my son returned to me to say that God was good or any other religious sentiment, it would not convince me of his presence; but if he says that I once played cricket against his Eton team in two right-foot boots, then he gives me a trvial thing which proves to me his own identity.

I then made a counter-attack, pointing out that psychical

research meant the study of the soul, that it was endorsed by Gladstone, Balfour, and many of the greatest minds, that the knowledge of the soul was the special job of the bishops and clergy, and yet that as far as I knew no bishop belonged to any Psychical Research Society the whole world over, save only one in Iceland. Their job was taken over entirely by laymen, and instead of help we had ignorant opposition from those whose real duties we were doing. I wonder when the leaders of the Churches will wake up to the absurdity of the position and understand the immense responsibility which they have incurred.

Our Sunday service was a great success, and the Hall was crammed in spite of a severe storm. Mr. Lloyd, the head of the local Spiritualists, took the chair with dignity. Ashton Jonson read St. Paul's chapter on the gifts of the spirit, which brought home to the people how closely the early Christian Church was united to our modern views. For my own part I abandoned the eternal talk about proofs, which can never be proofs to those who are too careless to examine them, but I spoke upon our doctrinal aspects, and especially towards our relations to the Christ, which is the question which is likely to break us in two. It is better, however, to be broken in two than to avoid that which is so crucial. I said that while we scraped the barnacles off the boat we must not scrape also a hole in the bottom of it. Because the

Churches had made a sad mess of it that was no reason to abandon the Christ, but rather to try and understand and proclaim His true position, for the more we stripped Him of the ecclesiastical and the mystical, and the more we recognized Him as a high spirit sent by God for our enlightenment, differing in degree but not in kind from other high spirits, the more lovable and admirable He became. I showed also how His death was a mere incident, common to many reformers, but His life was really that upon which our attention should be fixed, and that there was no warrant at all for making Him the scapegoat for our sins. Let every man bear his own burden and pay his own debt. That is the teaching of the spirit world.

After my address that remarkable medium, Mrs. Kimpton, who did so well at Cape Town, gave the clairvoyance. She was splendid, but the audience was unaccustomed to see miracles wrought in their presence and was awed but unresponsive, so that it was difficult to get acknowledgments of many of her successes. The people addressed sat like dummies and would not respond. Afterwards they came round in several instances to apologize, and to say that they were so dumbfounded to hear their family names and secrets given out that they did not know what to do. One man had a message from his mother, name given correctly with many details. He told us afterwards that he had not

133

heard from his mother for nine months, but had no reason to think she was dead. If now he hears by normal means of her death, it will certainly be a remarkable case.

There was a war dance on Sunday, in the morning, which was organized by the City Deep Mine. The performers were Shangaans, who are natives from the Portuguese Territory. It was certainly a remarkable performance, into which the actors, at least 100 in number, put tremendous energy and vigour, so that only well-trained athletes could have carried it through. With shields and imitation assagais they fought all sorts of skirmishes and battles in most realistic fashion. There was a touch of epilepsy, I thought, in the excitement and contortions of some, of the warriors. The band, clad like a football team in red-and-white jerseys, played with great rhythm and melody upon some queer instruments, known as Kaffir pianos. Their sense of time was wonderful, and on the whole the music gave me more pleasure than the performance. It ended with "God save the King," and without a collection, so that it was art for art's sake with these poor negroes.

One more excursion was undertaken before we left Johannesburg. It was to the Premier Diamond Mine, which involved a trip of 130 miles or so, much of it over very rough roads. It was a tiring excursion, but well worth doing in spite of its unfortunate sequel to myself.

The mine is the biggest hole in the ground ever yet dug by man, and it literally made one gasp when one looked down into it and saw men like ants crawling about at the bottom, against a background of bluish soil. It is in this soil, hardened to rock, that the diamonds are found, though why it should be so is still a puzzle. The procedure is to blast a whole long line of the rock, to put the broken-off chunks into little trucks, to run the trucks down to the machines, and there to smash them up until they are mere gravel, at which stage the diamonds are extracted. As we looked down into the abyss the blasting began – several tons of dynamite being exploded in many different shots. First we saw the smoke of the fuses, then we saw the little figures all running for shelter, and then a dead silence until the first crash, followed by volleys of them, more like a barrage in the Great War than anything I have seen. The instant the silence was resumed out rushed the little figures, and were tugging and hauling to get the debris into the trucks, for they are paid by results, and a Kaffir can earn as much as 12*s*. or 15*s*. a day, which is an enormous wage in his eyes. It was a very animated scene. A wire cage runs on a steel rope down into the pit, and we all went down in this so as to get a closer view and finally returned in it to the surface. The place where the great Cullinan diamond was excavated was shown to us, but even moderate stones seem to be rare, and though we saw quite a large handful which had been cleared up that day, there was none which could not have been set in an ordinary ring.

It was a great day but tiring – too tiring for me. I had been in a great strain for six weeks and breaking time had come. However, it only took the form of a sharp attack of gastro-enteritis which laid me by the heels for three days. I have always boasted that since I took up my active work for Spiritualism I have never spent a day in bed, though travelling at all seasons in so many lands. This was my sharpest attack, but my record is still unbroken, for I was able even at the worst to sit in the sitting-room and dictate occasional letters and see visitors. It was a hard thing, however, that just then we had to lose our two admirable helpmates and companions, Charles Ashton Jonson, and Ethel his wife, who had each done so much to ease our work. They went South to Cape Town, and we North via Mafeking to Bulawayo. We were sad indeed to leave them. At the station a great crowd of friends had assembled to see us off, and so at last we bade farewell to Johannesburg, where we had met some of the dearest souls that we have ever yet encountered.

No one can leave Johannesburg without some speculation as to the future of so remarkable a town, which has sprung into its full-blooded, noisy life within the space of forty years. I have already given the reasons which make one alarmed as to that future. Even if the reef does not give out, it is already clear that the paying portion of it will be elsewhere and the central portion deserted. It seems to me that it would be wise for the city, while there is yet time, to develop some other world-wide industry, in which it would be helped by the presence of all those sources of power which already exist. What seems to me most natural would be a large meat-canning and fruit-canning development. The town has the illimitable veld around it; there is no limit to the herds and flocks which could be bred there. The railways are propitious. Labour is cheap. The products could be shipped without more expense than the products of Chicago. I speak as an ignorant man, but it seems to me that the ultimate salvation of Johannesburg might lie in that direction. And now adieu, you City of Gold. There are better things than gold, and may I have helped you to find them. To-morrow a new reel opens in the cinema of life.

CHAPTER VII

Bechuanaland – The Khami Ruins – The Matoppo Hills – A
Psychic Interlude – The Victoria Falls – The Rain Forest –
Livingstone's Journal – A Rhodesian Farm – Bitter Political
Feeling – General Prospects of Rhodesia.

It is a wearisome journey of two nights and a day –
nearly 600 miles – from Jo'burg to Bulawayo, but we
found it less trying than we had expected. The train was
slow but comfortable, and the line was so good that one
could write without extreme difficulty. The first
morning found us at historical Mafeking. Then for a
long day we traversed Bechuanaland, with the legendary
Kalahari Desert upon our left, in which some of our scientific men think that life originated. It is a huge waste
now, in which a few Bushmen lead a mysterious existence. I hope the time will come when the artesian well
will change all that and the wilderness may blossom. At
present it is rather the other way, and the area of desert
seems inclined to come east and south so as to involve
the Karoo. Every one agrees that the country grows
drier and droughts more common.

We stopped at many little wayside stations where the Bechuanas brought down rude wooden figures of animals for sale. I amused them by doing some conjuring tricks with them from the open carriage window, and they stared open-eyed when they saw a little wooden crocodile scamper up my arm. I expect I have introduced a new occupation into Bechuanaland, and that many will try to acquire the art. Women sell bottles of milk and fruit at these stations, but the milk is to be avoided, for has not the vivacious author of that excellent book *Sally in Rhodesia* narrated that she saw a nursing mother replenish a half-emptied bottle from her own natural store. Ugh!

It has an attraction of its own, that vast Kalahari Desert, to which I have alluded so casually. The huge tract is inhabited only by a few tribes of wandering Bushmen, the survivors of a race which once stretched from the caves of Northern Spain to those of Rhodesia, or even farther South. They are peaceable enough, these poor people, most miserable of the human race; but the land has to be policed, and patrols are sent out upon camels. This Bechuanaland police are a curious body, comprising some 30 Europeans and 250 natives. It is a deadly land. Once in 1879 a well-equipped body of Boers trekked across it, but they left their oxen and their wagons upon the face of the desert and they hardly escaped with their lives. The police, however, are used to its conditions, and they with their camels perform extraordinary journeys. The camels only need watering every fifth day, and the record is held by a policeman and camel who travelled without water, the man for three and the camel for twelve days. Both were laid up by over-indulgence when they came to the wells. A party recently with motors went right across the Kalahari, covering 500 miles. To their amazement they found in the centre a large tract of land, the Mecca of the Bushmen, as fertile as the best land in Africa. I hope it will be long before the poor little people are driven out of their last refuge.

The second morning found us at Bulawayo, which has now some 30,000 inhabitants, 7,000 of which are white. We were amazed to find what a young giant it was, with its broad streets and fine shops, which would do credit to any English provincial town. The Grand Hotel presents every reasonable comfort to the traveller. As our time was limited and we wanted to see the Victoria Falls, we started sightseeing at once, and set off that very afternoon in the care of Mr. Vincent, the theatre representative, who showed us great courtesy and attention. The Khami Ruins, some 14 miles from the town, were our destination.

These are of the same class as the great Zimbabwe Ruins and present the same mystery. There are remains of a considerable city and the walls are built of squared stone without mortar. There are no signs or inscriptions of any kind. I have examined a great many implements found on this or similar sites, and none of them present any signs of civilization. They vary from stone neolithic weapons to copper and finally to iron spear-heads and axes, but at no time would it seem that a cultured race occupied the ground. At the same time curious signs of trade intercourse with distant regions crop up. I observed a broken Nankin Chinese plate and some chips of undoubted Venetian glass. Malcolm got a huge scorpion from under a stone and cunningly enticed it into his killing bottle. It was the one living inhabitant which we saw in what was once a great city.

> "They say the lion and the lizard keep
>   The Courts where Jamshyd gloried and drank deep;
> And Bahram, that great hunter, the wild ass
>   Stamps o'er his head, and he lies fast asleep."

These Khami Ruins are certainly much more recent than the Great Zimbabwe temple and fort. The general idea as put forward by the most recent authorities is that the whole of this ancient civilization and industry may be divided into two quite distinct epochs, the first being the Zimbabwe Period, when a civilized race built fine buildings and introduced really workmanlike methods of mining. Then came a second period associated with the Portuguese exploitation, when only the outcrops were worked in a very superficial way and buildings were much less finished than before. The Ancient Period may have dated from 800 B.C., that figure being very elastic. The latter period was from 1400 onwards. The whole question is most debatable, and various authorities, Bent, MacIvor, Hall and others, rage furiously together. Nothing but a thorough digging will ever solve the various problems presented by the ruins.

The dates form one problem, and the people form the other. Who were these ancient workers? There are various schools, each of whom present arguments which they claim to be conclusive. One set believe that they were Indians, and point to the bird of Vishnu engraved upon the stones, to phallic emblems, to Indian plants, with various other signs of Indian occupation. Then there is the Sabean school, who claim that the old miners were from Southern Arabia. They certainly knew how to build, for even now it is hardly possible to fit a penknife between the stones of Zimbabwe. This puts out of court a third school, who contend that the Bantu Kaffirs built the whole thing. This seems to me to be an utterly untenable idea. One friend[1] who has studied the matter excited my imagination by a declared resemblance between the measurements and design of Zimbabwe and of the original Temple of Solomon as given in the Bible. "The Phœnicians built the one and so surely the Phœnicians built the other," said my friend. It is an alluring theory, but I cannot find many facts to support it.

[1] This lady, Miss Bayley, deserves mention as one of the Intellectuals of Jo'burg, and as having established at Roedean a famous centre of female education.

The reason for these walled towns, which are found in all parts of Rhodesia, is plainly that they should be centres for the ancient gold-miners, and possibly forts, for protection against the natives. The old gold diggings are usually found not far off, though strangely enough in the case of the chief town, Zimbabwe, there are none in the immediate neighbourhood. It was probably a central depot or collecting station, and there are traces of a line of block-houses which protect an old road from there to the point of shipment at Sofala. Thence the gold is usually supposed to have gone to Ophir in Southern Arabia, and then on to Phœnicia, and the world at large. It is reckoned that not less than 100 million pounds worth of gold have been taken out, so that it probably formed a considerable proportion of the old-world supply.

The portion mined has been very thoroughly gutted, but luckily for modern investors and for Rhodesia itself the ancients had no pumps; and when on the 100-foot level they struck water, as they usually did, they abandoned the mine. The most successful mines in the country now are continuations of these abandoned workings. There was one curious point which was confirmed to me by two separate observers, namely that some of the stopes or rock cuttings are only 18 inches wide and yet have been worked. No ordinary man could find room to wield a pick there, so the inference is that the workers of old were enslaved Bushmen, who were small enough to fit into such a crevice. It is a curious problem why the whole place with its flourishing industry should have been suddenly and utterly abandoned. The probable reason, I think, is that the first wave of the fierce virile Bantu, the ancestors of Zulus, Matabeles, and all fighting negroid tribes, came down from the North and cleared the country. This would probably be in the early Middle Ages, and then wave after wave followed, who exterminated the aborigines, and would have utterly conquered the whole of Africa had they not at last met the Dutch and the British coming up from the South. The assagai then, though it beat the bow, was no use against the musket.

To-day, Sunday, January 13th, we have just returned from an excursion which will stand out as one of the most memorable of our very varied experiences. It was to the Matoppo Hills to see the grave of that strange but very great man, Cecil Rhodes, a mighty leader, a man of broad vision, too big to be selfish but too determined not to be unscrupulous – a difficult man to appraise with our little human yard-sticks. Just as some souls are heaven-sent upon the spiritual side, the Buddhas and Christs of the world, so others are sent from on high with special practical missions, the Joan of Arcs, the Napoleons, the history-makers of all sorts. Heaven-sent was Cecil Rhodes, and heaven-guarded above all human institutions is that British Empire which he did so much to extend. I am convinced that who works for it works in a broad sense for God, for amid human errors and backslidings it does in the main, more than anything upon earth, stand for the God-like attributes of duty, justice, law, order, and toleration.

The grave is 27 miles from Bulawayo, and as you return by another route you traverse some 60 miles of country, most of it the same scrub-covered veld which covers most of the 500 miles from Mafeking northwards. Fantastic rocks, granite for the most part, split and piled in grotesque heaps, rose up before us and gradually assumed the dignity of hills. These are the historical Matoppos, which extend for 100 miles by 40, a labyrinth of craggy precipices, huge overhanging boulders, sudden caves, and mysterious valleys. It is a nightmare country and so impenetrable that no troops could get the Matabele out from it in the 1896 campaign, and it was only by surrounding it and cutting off all supplies that the brave savages were at last subdued and consented to meet Rhodes and discuss terms of peace.

At last our cars – we had two – came to a halt, and a brown path leading up through the thick green bushes was pointed out to us as the road we should take. It was midday and blazing hot, but we trudged along, our attention continually drawn to the beautiful butterflies, moths and beetles which flew past. Many of them found their last home in Malcolm's big green net and killing bottle. Funny little lizards with blue or red heads darted over the scorching rocks. They must have asbestos stomachs! Once the boys put up an iguana, 2 or 3 feet long, which escaped down a crack in the rock. The last we had seen was near Brisbane in Australia. Surely the distribution of animals is one of the great unsolved mysteries of creation.

The green scrub thinned away and we found ourselves on bare, curving, rather slippery rocks. Up these we clambered, and then, far above us against the deep blue tropical sky, we saw a bare, bald hill-top with a coronet of great round boulders like some prehistoric circle. This we knew to be our destination. It was hard and hot going, but we persevered, and so at last we found ourselves upon the hill-top, within that sacred circle of huge stones, and at the side of the simple iron slab which said, "Here lie the remains of Cecil Rhodes." What a dramatic resting-place for a great man! From it we could see a hundred miles of the land which his energy and foresight had rescued from savagery and brought under the flag of our country. So far as the eye could reach those wonderful hills, brown or red in the foreground and blue in the distance, stretched away, ridge after ridge, to the horizon. It matters not to the soul of Cecil Rhodes where his old body-coat may lie, but it is an inspiration to the land which bears his name that even it, the poor instrument which once he used, should be part of their soil.

And here I must leave the ways of the casual traveller, and speak for a moment of that which may be very alien to the minds of some of my readers. I expect, however, that any who are antagonistic to my views have long since parted company with me. I would say then that I had a psychic message from Rhodes when I was in Cape Town, saying that if I went to his grave he would have something to say to me. "A proof of his presence" was the exact phrase. Such messages often come and are discounted or disregarded, but this particular one came from Mrs. Kimpton, for whose powers I had a well-founded respect. She had visited Groote Schuur, Rhodes' old house, and while there had seen both Rhodes and Kruger, these two great shades, in very friendly colloquy. They had discussed my mission, Rhodes giving a very hearty blessing and Kruger a sonorous "Amen", which seemed to show that he has now burst the strait-jacket of the Dopper Church to which he belonged. Then followed the assignation to which I allude.

We stood in reverent thought for some time by the grave, and I then with my quartz-lensed camera, which is supposed to have a broader psychic radius than crystal, took several photographs, making different combination groups, in the hope that psychic power of that rare quality which affects the plate might be found among us. In this I may say, that we were entirely disappointed. I then asked my wife to sit with her pencil and

148

paper upon the low granite parapet which surrounds the grave. For some time we had no success. At last, however, her hand was strongly agitated and she wrote a few words. The power then died away and we had almost despaired, when it came again in full gush, and she wrote rapidly to the end, with short pauses for my interpositions. My trouble is that this Rhodes message was so kindly to myself and to my work that I may not reproduce it in full. It was fairly long, but there was some which I may transcribe, and it will be found in the Appendix for those who take an interest in such matters.

With a charming courtly message to my wife the writing came to an end. Nothing really evidential there, Mr. Critic. Only that throb and beat of truth which carry conviction at the time and place.

The old Kaffir guardian of the place had watched our strange proceedings as if fascinated. I wonder what he knew. When we rose he saluted my wife with a long, sustained salutation.

One has to disregard the laughter of fools, the crackling of thorns under the pot, when one writes of such episodes as this. But the thorns crackle, as it seems to me, less loudly. What is there incredible in such a situation, when the novelty of the thought has once been overcome – that novelty which is the first barrier to every fresh truth? Is telepathy between incarnate minds not a common phase to every man who has studied the subject? And would telepathy not be much easier where one mind, and that a very vigorous one, was untrammelled by the limitations of matter? Why should not such a mind project thought into a suitable receiving-station which is on that correct corresponding vibration without which no contact can be effected? Look at it from that point of view and you will find nothing intrinsically absurd, but you will get an explanation for much which can be explained in no other fashion. The world has to enlarge its ideas before it can realize the great change that has arrived.

To return to mundane things: Jameson's grave lies beside his leader's, but on a lower level as is but right and proper. Then hard by is the monument to Alan Wilson, who with forty brave comrades was cut off in the Shangani fight. It is very well done, but it is ill placed and the four decorative panels are too alike in treatment. At least one, if not two, should have been devoted to the actual battle. On the other hand, each panel is in itself a work of art. My own opinion is that even now the authorities would be wise to remove Mr. Tweed's monument to the Central Park of Bulawayo, where a thousand would see it for one who can reach it now.

This lonely grave is a wonderful place by day. But what must it be by night? Then even the single Matabele watcher is withdrawn and there is no human being within miles. The leopard roams over the plateau and leaves his spoor and his droppings in the red dust beside the iron slab. Down below in the matted jungle night-birds cry, and the terrible African snakes, the green mamba of the trees and the dark mamba of the earth, writhe among the tangled shrubs. It is real wild nature, the very heart and soul of Africa, which sheds its atmosphere round the solitary tomb.

We made our slow way downhill, lunched at the cars, and then drove back, full of thought and memories, to the rising city which so few years ago was the head kraal of a bloodthirsty savage. It was a great day, and I sit now in the evening putting it on record lest the memory of details slip from my mind.

Having done the Khami Ruins on the day of our arrival, and the Matoppo Hills upon the next day, we started upon Monday, January 14th, for the Victoria Falls, which was rather strenuous going for an invalid and did not improve my complaint. However, I have nearly a week in which to convalesce, as I do not address Bulawayo till next Sunday. It is a 250-mile journey, but it is worth it. The train runs through unbroken country, and all evening we were peering out of the window looking for wild animals. Some ostriches, a feline creature like a lynx, and several sable antelopes, which looked like large shaggy goats, exhausted our list, but we heard wondrous tales of pythons and elephants. In the morning I was up early and was looking over the great expanse of green foliage which lay rather under the level of the line when I saw a strange sight. For a mile or more a huge cloud of smoke was rising over the trees. "Surely," I thought, "we have here the father of all Forest Fires." And then suddenly it dawned upon me. This was the spray of the Falls, and we had reached our destination.

Having breakfasted at the hotel, we made our way down to the great bridge which spans the Rapids – a very remarkable engineering feat, and the highest bridge of the sort in the world. From it one sees part of the Falls, but it is not impressive, and those who only see it from railway-carriage windows as they pass have a very imperfect idea of the whole. The Rapids beneath are not imposing and cannot compare with the terrific rush and swirl of the Niagara Gorge. Thus our first feeling was one of disappointment. At the other side of the bridge we found ourselves in Northern Rhodesia, which is entirely independent of that which we usually call Rhodesia. It is still a Crown Colony whereas the other, as stated, has Responsible Government. No doubt they will be united in time. At present there are only 5,000 white inhabitants and a very large black population in the Northern province, the chief towns of which are Livingstone and Broken Hill. The chief gold-mines are in the South, but it is in the North that the huge copper deposits are found, which are so large and so accessible that good judges have declared that Northern Rhodesia is destined to be the chief source of the world's supply in the not too distant future.

On our second day at the Falls we had two excursions, one of which was very pleasant, while the other might have ended in tragedy. For the first we got up early and visited the Rain Forest, which skirts the Falls, and which is for ever drenched with their spray. I suppose it is one of the few places upon earth where night and day, and century after century, it has never for one instant ceased to rain. It would of course be impassable bog if it were not that the rock is near the surface. The result is a prodigious growth of vegetable life, but from end to end I saw no living thing. I suppose the lower animals don't care about perpetual rain more than we should.

The edge of the Forest is a chasm which faces the Falls, and as you walk along there are many projections and promontories on which you stand and admire. I can see now that the glimpse which we had yesterday from the railway bridge is quite deceptive and that the real Falls are infinitely greater. When you are in the thick of it, the roar and crash and smoke of it are so awful that I could quite understand some weak-minded creature losing hold of himself and casting himself into the chasm.

It is very much larger in every way than Niagara – indeed, a modest American has recorded that Niagara is a mere perspiration beside it. At the same time I doubt if there is any single point so impressive as the Horseshoe Fall on the Canadian side. But then there are a dozen points nearly as great. No words can give any idea of the terrific majesty and power of it, and it has the enormous advantage over all such sights, that it stands, and will stand in virgin Nature, without a house visible upon either bank. The hotel, which is charmingly built and well run, stands discreetly back and never offends the eye. There is only the hotel and one or two little curio stores – nothing else save the township of Livingstone, capital of Northern Rhodesia, which is some 9 miles on the other side of the Falls.

The second excursion to-day was undertaken by the youngsters alone, as I am still on the sick-list. It was to a place called the Palm Gorge. They got down to this place, which is near the banks of the river, when a tropical thunderstorm came on with terrific rain, a real cloud-burst. The path by which they had come down was converted into a raging torrent, against which they had to struggle knee-deep in their effort to get back. Had they lost their footing, the consequences would have been tragic. Both the boys declare that Billy behaved according to the highest traditions of the Girl Guides, an association of which she is an enthusiastic member. Their mother had a vivid presentiment of their danger, but all ended well when three bedraggled figures appeared at last on the veranda. Thank God and all ministering spirits that it was no worse. We are continually conscious of protection around us.

I have been reading *Livingstone's Journal and Life*, which is appropriate here since he discovered the Falls in 1855, and has given his name to the near-by town. He certainly was a very perfect Christian gentleman. I was struck by the fact that, in spite of his Scotch theology, he seemed to have some instinctive knowledge of psychic truth – more so than was usual in the stodgy age in which he lived. When in danger of death, he thinks of his children and quotes the lines:

> "I shall look into your faces
>   And listen to what you say,
> And be often very near you
>   When you think I'm far away! –"

which is indifferent verse but very sound Spiritualism. He tells us how he used to hear the wretched slaves singing some verses with a hilarity which amazed him so much that he asked what they meant. They translated them as meaning that when they died their spirits would come back to haunt and to kill those who had so ill-used them. Livingstone seems to accept the idea. I have no doubt myself that those who have been brutally used have at long last certain weapons against their oppressors which are not yet fully recognized. When they are, perhaps the cruel will be more careful in their actions. It is recorded in *Red*

Russia that a particular form of madness ending in death used to break out among the executioners of the Soviets, and that the sufferers died from insomnia, raving that they saw their victims all around mocking and gibbering at them. None are so helpless that they may not have some means of revenge – even if it be nobler not to use it.

My continued indisposition prevented me from enjoying this wonderful place as much as I would otherwise have done. I was too weak to get about with comfort. Wild life is very close to you, however, for from the portico of the hotel I saw a troop of nine baboons, prowling about for what they could find. I made one expedition up the river and had distant views of one or two crocodiles, with a fair variety of bird life, including a great number of the pretty white parrot-like bird which furnishes the aigrette of commerce.

The boys went up later in a canoe, and Malcolm actually shot a crocodile, but as it was at long range with an automatic pistol I don't suppose the creature was much the worse.

The Falls will always remain a pleasant memory, in spite of my ill-health, for the place is unique both in scenery and in the comfort of the hotel. Duty called us, however, and Sunday morning, January 20th, found us back in Bulawayo with a lecture to do that night. I was rather pulled down, but I have always found that once I am on the platform the needed strength is freely given. So it proved, and the lecture went excellently well. Seldom have I had a more intelligent and sympathetic audience.

Our last day in Bulawayo was spent in visiting and examining a typical Rhodesian farm of the smaller kind – though 3,500 acres would not seem small from a home standpoint. It is run by Mr. Harding Forrester, whose novel about Rhodesia, *Sowers on the Dust*, is an excellent picture of one side of the life of the country. We, who had so lately undergone it, thought that the description of the voyage was a remarkable *tour de force*. I fancy that literature rather than farming will absorb Mr. Forrester's future energies, but at present he is quite content with his broad acres. The farmhouse was built by the family with their own hands – which means, I fancy, in South Africa by the hands of their negroes. It is 10 miles from the town, and it sustains some 200 cows, which furnish milk and butter for Bulawayo. Sheep are a side line. Many acres of mealies have been cultivated to feed the cattle, and have to be stored in silos for the winter. When the mealies fail through locusts, want of water, or other causes, the cattle die and the farmer too often is ruined. It is a gamble – like farming all the world over. However, Forrester values his farm now at a substantial sum, and he bought it at little over prairie prices, so in spite of a certain vein of pessimism in his books there is still a good life and a decent profit to be had in Rhodesia.

There were neighbours there, and the conversation ran upon the urgent topic of Union with their big neighbour to the South. There are considerable economic advantages, but the racial question dominates them. They will not take the chance of coming under an anti-British Government. They all trust and admire Smuts, but they fear the Nationalists. It is very much the same situation as exists in Ireland, where the North has every economic reason to unite with the South, but cannot bring itself to make common cause with those who are out of sympathy with all their racial traditions and time-honoured loyalty. But time will work wonders in both cases.

One of the first remarks made to me by a Rhodesian – a hard-bitten ex-officer – was: "I fought the Boers in 1900, and I think the feeling against them is stronger now than then." With the remark of the Johannesburg magnate in my mind, I took his observation more seriously than I would otherwise have done. "What is the cause of the feeling?" I asked. "The question of the flag and the persecution of the British. They have been turned out of their jobs continually to make room for Dutch. The language question, too, causes great irritation. How can we be expected to learn a barbarous patois which has no literature or roots of any kind, and is really a sort of slang Dutch?" So spoke the Colonel. Two others whom I have met since took an even graver view. If the flag question had not been compromised there would certainly have been violence, they say. I have little sympathy with these fire-eaters and I disagree about the flag; but I am bound to register the effect upon my own mind, which is that serious trouble may come of it. Perhaps if the South African or Moderate party win in the election which is due this year, it may ease the situation.[1]

I have not been long in Rhodesia, but I have traversed a good stretch of it, read all I could get and spoken with many who were in a position to know. I think that in time – say a century – it will be the very finest dominion that flies the British flag. It is enormous in extent. It has an equable climate. It has neither the winter of Canada, the deserts of Australia, the Maori question of New Zealand, nor the complex conditions of the South African Union. It is full of gold-mines, partly exhausted, it is true, by the ancients. It has in the North enormous copper deposits, and will probably produce as much and as cheaply as any in the world. It will grow tobacco, cotton, and many other commodities. Coal is common and good. Asbestos is found in quantities. The scrub and forest present no difficulty in clearing, as the timber is usually light. There is the one drawback, that there is no port of their own; but Beira on the East Coast and the Congo basin on the West are both accessible, and these

---

[1] But it was not so.

neighbours are not strong enough to be ever a menace. On the whole I know no dominion which is so happily situated.

The situation was very confusing whilst the land was governed by the Chartered Company, but that is partly over. Since 1923 Responsible Government has been granted. There were two parties, the Rhodesian who were moderate, and the Progressive who were in favour, so far as I understand it, of repudiating the claims of the Company altogether. This would be manifestly unjust, since the Company had founded the country and stood all the expense and dangers of the first settlement. It is good to know that the party which admitted this won the election and are now in power. If and when the country flourishes, the Chartered Company will have its fair but not exorbitant share of the profit.

The great issue which has been and will be before the electors is whether they should join the South African Union of States or remain aloof. General Smuts pleaded with passion that they should do so, and what that great man advises should have every attention and respect. But the generally disloyal and Republican attitude of the Dutch Nationalists has infuriated the Rhodesians to such an extent that they threw out the idea, and, so far as I can see, it has no chance of reconsideration for another generation. I met men who had been all for the Union and now were dead against it. Looked at from an Imperial point of view, there is an argument each way. If they joined the Union they would increase the weight of British representation there, which is badly needed. On the other hand, they represent, while they stand alone, a sort of insurance that, come what may, there is one solid block of British influence in South Africa. There is a tendency for the disgruntled British of the South to come North and take farms in Rhodesia. The general atmosphere is British and patriotic to an almost incredible extent. The mildest pro-Dutch argument is resented, and as to criticizing Rhodesia itself it would hardly be tolerated. Even when one disagrees, one loves these whole-hearted people. "If you don't like the country, there are two trains a day out of it." That is the answer to the querulous stranger.

At Bulawayo my wife repeated her views as to the hard lot of animals in South Africa, which brought about a deputation from the local Society, and a good deal of correspondence, ending with a long leader in the *Rhodesian Gazette*. On examination my wife was delighted to find that the Rhodesian Societies for Prevention of Cruelty were very active, and that the horses and mules here were in a very much better condition than in the Union. We have had a letter from Cape Town to say that there were no less than 1,200 cases in the courts since we left, so some progress should be made. In this humanitarian work, as in so many other ways, my wife has been of vital service in our mission.

There was some fine mixed theological fighting in Bulawayo during and after our visit, which ranged over the whole field of dogma and was not confined to Spiritualism. Archdeacon Mylne, Father Kendal, and others, attacked my views, but though they were united in their assault it was evident that they were deeply divided among themselves. Archdeacon Mylne, for example, declared that baptism was not now regarded among Christians as being necessary to salvation, which certainly would not be endorsed by a Roman Catholic priest. It really does seem absurd that Christians should set out to convert the heathen when they have not agreed among themselves what the Christian belief may be, so that they teach their converts to dislike and despise each other. All this would be avoided if all these close corporations and vested interests were dissolved and the simple tenets of the Christ – gentleness, kindness, and mercy – put in their place. A Chinese bishop told me once that all the Chinese Christian Churches of every sect would unite in a single generation if they were only left to themselves.

CHAPTER VIII

Chances in Rhodesia – Salisbury – A Remarkable House – Jan Ridd – The Umtali Murder – A Transvaal Case – Sally of Rhodesia – The Missions – A Personal Note – Farewell to Rhodesia.

To-day, January 23rd, we have traversed the 250 miles between Bulawayo, the business centre of Rhodesia, and Salisbury, the administrative centre. It is beautiful country, but it is amazing how undeveloped it is. A large part of it is reserved for natives, and you see the kraals in every direction. But of systematic cultivation we saw few traces in all that long journey until we came to extensive tobacco estates near the capital. The Rhodesian tobacco industry tempted many people out some years ago, but the boom was as usual overdone, with a bad reaction. Now it has settled down into its stride and means to stay. As an old pipe-smoker I should say that Rhodesian mixtures are pure and good, while Denis, who favours cigarettes, tells me that the "Rhodian" is an excellent smoke. It may give your baccy a better flavour if you feel that you are helping your overseas comrades.

Part of the country we traversed was magnificent savannah, a green carpet stretching unbroken to the blue line of the horizon. It seemed to me the most ideal grazing ground that I have ever seen, and yet there were few flocks or herds, and hardly ever a house. It is sad to think of all the poor fellows upon the dole at home, and then of this huge land calling out for cultivation. It is always the same question of capital that blocks the way. In the Cape Union they have no use for the man with less than £2,000, and that is an absolute minimum. But I hear better accounts here. They say that a real hard-working young couple with a few hundred pounds and some State help, which is usually to be had, could get their roots in and make good, but it needs pluck and patience, and a home market can only be found when there is an industrial population. I have wondered whether Government could not keep a small staff of experts, one of whom could be told off to mother each new family which settles on the land, if it were only for a few weeks. He would say to them: "Now, here is your land. It is in this corner that your home should be. Your water supply comes here. Your best crops would be so and so." This would help the newcomer enormously, and a small charge upon the farm, to be paid later, would cover the expense.

The claims of the Chartered Company still tangle up the mineral rights. But now that self-government has been gained, that should be gradually set right. But the new-comers must deal fairly with the old shareholders. Things will never be right until the Chartered Company has been bought out and the capital sum taken over as a State debt. The interest should not be crushing, and the country would be freed from this liability which cripples its development.

Salisbury is a young giant in an even earlier and less developed period of growth than Bulawayo. They are both planned on a large scale with broad streets and magnificent distances, but it must be many years before they fulfil their promise. The shops of Bulawayo are supreme and there is a general air of activity which is distinctive, but Salisbury is the Government centre, and has a larger cultured class, who live in the charming homesteads which extend in every direction round the town. Many of the citizens have their houses miles out in the country, so that they can have small home farms of their own. This was the case with Judge McIlwaine, who with his charming Irish wife offered us every hospitality. Driving out to him, we were pleased to see a fine silver jackal, like a large fox, standing near the road. On this same road only a few years ago a lion suddenly put in an appearance, so Salisbury is not very far removed from wild nature. Her future citizens will read of such things with the same amazement that Londoners feel when they learn from Macaulay that woodcocks were once shot in Maida Vale.

We were taken to see a truly remarkable house, Rumbavu, by name, which lies about 8 miles from Salisbury. It was erected by a Mr. Peech, who was connected with the steel industry, and as he desires now to sell or let it I might be of some use in describing it. Both my wife and I thought it was the most fascinating place we had ever seen. It occupies the top of a kopje, which has been terraced all the way down to make a wonderful garden full of surprises. The house itself, which is made of stone, is quite original, of no known form of architecture, but extraordinarily effective and convenient. The view is wonderful. With a good library there, and with Salisbury within easy motor run, I could not imagine a more wonderful retreat for a man of studious and retiring habits who wished to get away from the world and yet to have it at call when needed.

I found Salisbury to be much in advance of the average British town in psychic knowledge – thanks to the work of Judge McIlwaine, Colonel Hope Carson, and other citizens. I gave their Psychic Society an evening which was, I hope, mutually instructive and pleasant. Several promising amateur mediums are in different stages of development. Certainly our knowledge is now catholic in the sense that no nation is without it. At the recent congress over which I presided in London forty-one nations sent messages and twenty-six were actually represented, some of them by considerable deputations. The Icelander sat by the Bolivian, and the Slav by the Japanese. One of the best speeches was by a negro. The Japanese seem to be especially advanced in psychic truth. Smiler Hales, in the record of his life, says: "Japan's greatness rests not upon the sword, but upon the people's faith in the spirit life. In Japan no one dies – folks just put aside their bodies as we put aside our clothing when we go to sleep. The spirit goes on with its life after what we call death much as it did on earth. A 'dead' father can look after the honour of the family he begat – he can comfort and help. I have smiled at English impudence which sent missionaries to meddle with the faith of the East." Quite so, but if ahead of us in truth and knowledge, they may be behind in ethics and civilization, which are quite separate. We have each something to teach the other. I remember that when I was at Vancouver I was told that the Japanese fishermen were amazed at the ignorance of the Anglo-Saxons in matters of the spirit. The finest instance that I can remember of the practical everyday matter-of-course working of spirit intercourse was when, at the end of the Japanese-Russian War, Togo stood upon a hillock on the seashore and called his dead sailors around him, saying that it was only their due that he, their Admiral, should announce to them the terms of peace for which they had fought. They knew them already, of course, but it was a supreme official act of courtesy. How unreal and futile all our celebrations seem when compared with this!

We took up our quarters at Meikle's Hotel, which is remarkably well run and comfortable. We were never better housed.

Here, a day or two after our arrival, we had a visit from Jan Ridd as near as the modern world can produce him, in the person of John Hopley, International Rugger player and Champion Amateur Heavyweight, whose record has never been beaten. When he won the public school championship he already weighed 13 stone 7 pounds, and later I should think he was not far short of 16 stone of hard muscle. I met him first at the National Sporting Club in war-time. He and his brother ran a great farm near here. They tossed which should go the War. John lost, but when the brother was killed John let the farm mind itself and set forth to take his brother's place. That was twelve years ago, but Jan Ridd is as big and strong as ever. He is a true South African, half British, half Dutch, but he is averse from joining the Union until the loyalty of the Nationalists is more certain. His farm is 29,000 acres – an enormous estate – mostly cattle, and he tells me that if he had all the wealth of the world it is still as a Rhodesian farmer that he would live and die. With such sentiments wise politicians would make some use of so remarkable and wholehearted a man. Other men of note whom we met were the Governor Sir Cecil Rodwell, a very courteous gentleman, and the Prime Minister Moffat, a hard-headed Scot, the grandson of the famous missionary and explorer of the same name. The Prime Minister told me that he regarded the native question as the most important, and that he was working for a system of local councils by which they should be part of the Government and so be more immune to Bolshevist influence.

A very extraordinary Rhodesian crime to which my attention was drawn was the Umtali murder, which presented some features which seem to me unique, and which would have rejoiced the heart of my old friend Churton Collins, who was a connoisseur in such matters. Put briefly, the case stood thus: In Umtali, which is a small town near the Rhodesia-Portuguese border, there was an Englishman named Winter who was putting in a short wait until the steamer should arrive at Beira, which would convey him on his lawful occasions to India. He stayed at the Royal Hotel, and there was nothing against him or his record – a friendly, harmless sort of man, forty-four years of age, with wife and family in England. In the same small town was a woman – Miss Knipe – who was engaged at the local stores, forty-three years of age, with no physical attractions and no particular quality, save that she was remarkably strong – as muscular as a man. She also had a room at the Royal Hotel. This middle-aged couple never met until November 5th, 1928, and on the evening of November 6th they went for a little walk in the Umtali Park, a large, ill-lighted place with occasional seats. The woman was of good character, the man was sober, they were new acquaintances; it did not seem a promising opening for a most dramatic sequel. What happened within the next hour is a problem which has vexed South Africa, and may continue well to do so.

It was after eight o'clock when the couple entered the Park. It chanced that another couple, a Portuguese named Lambeiro and an Irish girl, Miss O'Mahoney, sat courting on another bench which was not far off, but it was too dark for either couple to be aware of the other. At 8.45 a hooter blew which gave the exact time. Shortly after the girl deposed that she heard the sound of a quarrel, a confused noise, with a woman's and man's voice mingled. This lasted for some time. Then there was silence for some minutes. Then from the same direction came four distinct screams. The Irish girl, who seems to have been both brave and truthful, implored her companion to go and investigate, but he refused to do anything, and at the subsequent examination declared that he had never heard anything, which was so manifestly false that there was talk of a prosecution for perjury. Silence followed the screams, but after an interval she heard a man's voice calling for help three times in English. This would seem to have been shortly after nine. About 9.15 she saw three Kaffirs pass, with nothing remarkable in their demeanour. Shortly afterwards the couple left the Park, having made no further inquiry as to what had occurred.

There were several others who had heard the cries and who were less timorous. They were at a greater distance, however, in the homes which surrounded the Park, and it was some little time before they reached the spot. The first was one Kirkland. It was just after nine that he heard the cries, which fits in with the evidence of the previous witness. Rushing through the Park, he came upon the body of a woman, Miss Knipe, lying huddled across the path, quite dead, and bleeding from many wounds. There were no signs of criminal assault. He had an electric torch, and as he flashed it round he heard a voice in the dark say, "Here I am. I am knocked out." A man, who proved to be Winter, then rose from behind a tree, 25 yards away, and tottered towards him. He had blood on his face and seemed to be dazed and delirious. He kept repeating, "Who hit me? Who hit me?" He sat down on the grass as one exhausted.

Presently other people began to arrive, including a police constable, Rowe and afterwards Dr. Jackson. The man was removed to the hospital. He said, "Oh, doctor, don't take me to the hospital. Take me to the hotel. I have to catch my boat for India." Afterwards he said,

"You must have a madman running round loose here."

Let us now take Winter's own account of what had occurred. He said that Miss Knipe and he were sitting in perfect amity, the lady being upon his left. He had a recollection of seeing a native pass within 12 feet of him. He remembered nothing more until he came to his senses lying on the ground near the bench. Staggering to his feet, he looked round for his female comrade, missed her, staggered some 40 yards down the path and then came across the body. As it was pitch dark it was remarkable that he staggered in the right direction. He then collapsed again, and remembered no more until he found himself in the midst of the group who had come to the scene of the crime. Such is the account of Winter.

Now as to his injuries. They were most certainly not self-inflicted. His left jaw was cracked, and according to the medical evidence he had received three other heavy blows, one of which cut him behind the ear, and one near the eye. A heavy as well as an edged instrument seemed to have been used. It could hardly have been a knife. The sharper end of the head of a hammer would be more probable. No weapon of any kind was found near the seat of the murder, or on the person of either protagonist.

Now let us take the murdered woman's injuries. Her hands and forearms were cut to pieces in defending herself against repeated stabs from a knife. In addition there

were numerous cuts on the body, one of which had penetrated the lung, and a second the stomach. One cut was
in the back of the left shoulder. Death had been due to
loss of blood.

There is one other point which deserves to be noted.
There was a native hut 64 yards from the scene of the
crime. Two native women were in it, and gave their evidence in a very intelligent way, to the effect that after
the hooter blew they heard a woman's voice raised as if
in a quarrel, and that after this there came the screams.
This tale of a quarrel is confirmed by the previous evidence of the Irish girl, and is difficult to fit in with the
idea of a sudden stealthy attack.

Inspector Bond, who handled the case, seems to me to
have acted in a very intelligent way. He searched everywhere for a weapon, but found none – a most essential
point. He noted that the earth in front of the seat shows
signs of disturbance, but could find none at the back or
sides. He then traced drips of blood with two small
pools of blood along the path to the point where the
body was found – about 40 yards in all. The woman had
evidently backed away down the path screaming, while
her assailant had showered blows upon her, most of
which were caught upon her arms. She may have fallen
at the two points where the pools of blood were. There
was no indication of robbery.

These are the essential facts, so far as known. Winter

was arrested and charged with the murder, but Judge McIlwaine very wisely, as it seems to me, dismissed the case before trial. In the absence of motive, weapon, and evidence there could be no case for the prosecution. And yet what a perfect mystery the whole affair remains – more remarkable, I think, than any which a romancer could invent. What possible theory would cover the facts? How could Winter have assaulted the woman when he was himself in such evil case? And why should he assault her? And where was the weapon? Is it possible that in spite of her age she had a jealous admirer who assaulted Winter, and then when she turned upon him – hence the sound of quarrelling – made a murderous attack upon her. This is most unlikely, for there was no record of any such admirer. Or was there some homicidal maniac – native for choice – who might have attacked them? There was, it seems, an attack not entirely dissimilar some months before by a native. But would Winter have no recollection of it? And how came his injuries upon the left side of his head when the lady was seated to the left of him? It is to be remembered that blows upon the head sometimes remove the memory of events which led up to the blow, even to the extent of some minutes. That shadowy native, whom Winter says he saw, may have emerged and struck blows which left no trace in the memory. I confess that without further evidence I should be very loath to give an opinion. One conceivable theory is that the attack was not meant for this prosaic and middle-aged couple, but that in the dark the assailant chose the wrong people. It is even possible that the Portuguese and the Irish girl were the real objects of the vindictive hatred of some jealous rival. It is far-fetched, but within the bounds of possibility.

There is not much real crime in South Africa, either in the Union or in Rhodesia, though there is a very great deal of artificial crime depending upon the diamond monopoly and upon the laws relating to the natives. The only other unsolved mystery of first-class importance which came my way was that of Miss Kanthack's murder, which has already been alluded to. I refused to discuss this, though I was asked to give an opinion in the local Press, as it was a painful matter to revive. Writing from a distance, however, one may perhaps without offence say a little about the case, since it has already been so thoroughly ventilated. There was one feature of the crime which struck me as particularly remarkable, and that was the timing. The poor girl was seen approaching the fatal grove at 6.15 – at 6.30 her little dog arrived home in a bedraggled condition – at 6.35 her wristwatch had been shattered by a blow, and a little after 7 the alarm had been given, and there were searchers in the wood who failed to see the concealed body.

This is so remarkable that a persistent rumour got about that she had been abducted in a car, and then brought back next day and laid in the wood. This is quite inadmissible. It certainly was not so. The body was hid within a very few yards of the place where the poor girl had been slain, and had certainly never been anywhere else. That being so, we are presented with a curious problem. In a space of time which could hardly have been more than twenty minutes the criminal had been able to drag the body across, and then to cover it with such skill that for three days it lay hid, though Boy Scouts and others were hunting every yard of the wood. I would venture to draw two deductions from this. The first is that in all probability there were at least two criminals, since from what I saw of the undergrowth I should not think it possible for one man to have collected sufficient boughs and foliage to have covered the body in the time. It is a pity that it had rained heavily, for those boughs were certainly stained with fingerprints before they were washed off. My second deduction would be that the criminals were probably Europeans[1] or men of some brain power, who lived at a distance, and wanted time for getting away. A native living in a hut within a few hours' journey would naturally have made off and left the body. But if a man had a long motor or train journey before he would be in safety, it would mean everything to him to hide the body

[1] I see by to-day's paper, June 20th, that a European has been arrested.

so that there should be no general search and alarm before he got outside the danger zone. Those are the two points which struck me, but one is arguing from very insufficient data.

I must turn away, however, from the fascinating subject of criminology and get back to the problems of the country.

Owing to the Chartered Company complications the mining laws and customs in Rhodesia are most peculiar – so much so that they can hardly continue in their present form. We will suppose that you have a farm which is near some recognized gold reef or chrome deposit, or other source of mineral wealth. You look out of your window and you see gangs of men digging on your land and making trenches here and there without any reference to yourself. Ploughed land they may not touch, and they may not come nearer than 500 yards from the house, but otherwise they may do as they please. I heard of one man who had 50 miles of trenches dug at various times upon his farm. Whether they were left open or not I did not hear.

I have mentioned chrome, and I should have included it in the other products which make Rhodesia rich. It is used of course to harden steel, and it is essential for metal work which is exposed to much strain. Rhodesia has an absolute monopoly of it in the purer forms, though I understand that an inferior grade is found in South-Eastern Europe.

My lecture at Salisbury went remarkably well, and, as in Bulawayo, there was no vacant seat. I heard that many of the people had come a hundred miles by road to be present – and a hundred miles by road in this land of flooded spruits is no small matter. I saw cars there which were red up to the tops of their bonnets from the mud of rivers – cars which had clearly been dragged by ropes across the deep drifts. The fact is that many of these people had psychic experiences of their own, and had developed mediumistic powers in their lonely homesteads, and were now anxious to know more about the matter. That is where the literature which we distribute is so useful. It gives them a permanent reference. I find that we have left a trail of more than 2,000 books and pamphlets behind us. South Africa can never be quite the same. I should think that at the present moment its average of psychic knowledge is the highest of any community in the world.

On our last day in Salisbury we drove out to see the house in which Sally – the Sally of Rhodesia – lived. We had all been greatly captivated by the book which is a real human document, and as we sympathized with all Sally's joys and troubles we naturally wished to see the scene of them. We were driven some 4 miles out of the town and our guide took us to a small house on a rocky kopje. We got out of the car and proceeded to identify all the things she had mentioned – the jacaranda trees which she planted, the terrace, the tennis court, the view. We enthused over it all for ten minutes, at the end of which time our guide, who had gone indoors, returned with the information that it was the wrong house. After some search we did at last find the right one, but it was quite an anticlimax, and did not fit into our expectations nearly so well.

Nothing has surprised or depressed me more in this country than to find the almost universal lay opinion that the Missions of every sort have done more harm than good, and that the heathen natives are far more reliable and are on the higher scale of morality. I heard the same story from hotel people, from train people, from storekeepers, and from householders. Now and then a good Christian is reported, but it seems to be so rare that many employers refuse to engage any but raw natives. But how pathetic this is when one considers the efforts made both by those who supply the money at home and those who sacrifice their lives in the work. I put down this sad failure to the conflict of Christian creeds and to the attempt to teach dogma instead of simple ethics. If the savage was told something which was well within his powers of comprehension – if, for example, he was told that God sent a messenger named Jesus as an example to mankind and that to imitate Him we had to be gentle and merciful and unselfish – then if the white folk round followed the same precept, a great effect would surely be produced. The rest would be a matter rather of gradual civilization than of religion. But how can their poor simple minds understand all the complexities of the theologians or the obscurities and contradictions of the Bible?

As a corrective to the above passage I would add that I had a chat with the Rev. Glossop, who has been thirty-five years in Africa and is the head of the University Mission at Lake Nyassa. He is incidentally the brother of the Captain Glossop of the *Sydney* who sank the *Emden*. He admitted that there were many scallywags who called themselves Christians without any sanction. The best Christian boys, he said, remained with the Missions and did high-class civilized work as printers, carpenters, etc. This result could of course, as I pointed out, be reached without the aid of religion. He said, however, with some force that the missionaries were the moral police and that this discredited them in some quarters. I had every respect for Mr. Glossop personally, for he seemed a fine fellow; but I did not feel that his testimony met the almost universal disfavour with which the native Christian is regarded. The same applies often to the highly educated native. I was told of a case on the Rand where a brainy native became a fully qualified lawyer, and the first use he made of his powers was to go back to his native kraal and diddle his chief and his people out of their inheritance. One can only hope that an assagai put paid to his account.

I was amused lately in one of the endless public discussions upon psychic matters to see an attack upon my own judgment and power of forming a correct opinion upon evidence. It is difficult for a man to defend himself on such a point, as he might seem vainglorious if he quoted facts, and yet no one is in a position to quote them except myself. But the matter is important when the value of one's opinion in so vital a question is concerned, and so I will quote from memory a few of the instances in which I have interfered in public matters. Twice I have seen that verdicts were wrong and have persevered in the face of many obstacles until I got them reversed. I allude to the cases of George Edalji and Oscar Slater. I was the first in 1890 to warn the public from Berlin that Koch's treatment was by no means the certain cure that was imagined and to stop sufferers from swarming over. My letter appeared in the *Daily Telegraph*. In *The Times* I wrote at the time of the Boer War and suggested the Imperial Yeomanry before it was formed, and I also wrote in the same paper showing how a barrage could make a position, such as a kopje, indefensible and a death-trap. Thus I anticipated the fire tactics of the Great War. When I returned from the Boer War I had a controversy in *Cornhill* and other journals, in which I put forward certain military lessons from the War, nearly all of which have been justified. They included the forecast that no artillery would be so heavy

181

that it would not be used in the next war, that cavalry would be valuable as riflemen rather than as swordsmen, that an efficient army can be vamped up more quickly than orthodox opinion would admit, that rifle fire was everything, and that above all rifle clubs should be encouraged. Most of these contentions stood the test of time. When Queen Victoria died I wrote to *The Times* advocating the change in the Coronation oath which would delete the insult to Catholics. In this I anticipated what was actually done. Before the Great War I saw exactly how Germany would use her submarines against our food carriers, and had a story in the *Strand* to illustrate it, after sending memoranda in vain to the Navy and War Office. I attended and spoke at meetings for advocating the Channel tunnel, the neglect of which probably cost us 100 million pounds in the subsequent War. When war broke out I protested again and again in the Press against the want of lifebelts on men-of-war, and a rush order was given which provided every man with an inflatable collar. I worked for body armour for the troops, which materialized so far as head cover went.

I would add the Congo agitation and the attempt to reform our divorce laws as two other subjects at which I have worked, the first of them entirely successful, the latter commended by a Royal Commission.

These are a few of the points in which I have interfered in public affairs, and if I have given a prolonged blast upon my own trumpet the reader must forgive me, since my object is to ask him whether my views upon psychic matters are likely to be wild when on so many other subjects they have shown themselves to be judicious. The mere task of stating accurately the events of the Great War in historical form might, one might have hoped, vindicate one's judgment.

So now we bid farewell to Rhodesia and the Rhodesians. They are a gallant set of people, and more solid than I expected to find them from the impression I had gathered – through an analysis that was mostly from novels. I understood that they were hard drinkers, and so they are, the hardest I have ever met, but tea is their beverage. Tea when they are called, tea at breakfast, universal tea in every shop and office at eleven, tea again in the afternoon. As to liquor their sundowner habit has been criticized, but that is the malaria hour and their custom may be founded upon experience. They are a brave, cheery crowd, and the fiercest British patriots that I have ever encountered. As to their country, I see no limit to its future.

CHAPTER IX

A Giant's Playground – The Pungwe Marshes – Beira – A Cyclone – A Great Ray – Chicoa Silver Mines – The Gospel of St. John – Mandated Territory – Mombasa.

We have bad news as we hear that a section of the line connecting us with Beira has been washed away by the heavy rains. It is very serious, as our tickets are taken for the boat at Beira next Friday, which is to carry us to Mombasa. To catch it we have to start on Wednesday. I write on Tuesday morning, and we have no assurance of getting through. The break is in the Pungwe Marshes, in Portuguese territory – and it would be no joke for us all to be stranded in that mosquito-infested swamp. However, these floods go down as quickly as they rise, and we will hope for the best.

In the end the matter proved to be as dangerous as we had expected. Since it was a case of getting through or missing our boat, we took the chance. This bad washaway was confirmed as being at an unholy place, 40 miles from Beira, and we were told that no single train could possibly pass, though perhaps another train might pick us up at the farther side of the danger-point. We were compelled to sign an indemnity form to say that we took the risk and that in case of accident we would make no claim. Thus in the morning we steamed out of Salisbury, a knot of friends, including Judge McIlwaine and his wife, waving adieux in spite of the early hour.

It is an amazing stretch of country, the 200 miles which stretch from Salisbury to the Portuguese frontier. There are long tracts which are covered by such extraordinary collections of rocks, piled upon each other, that my wife remarked that it might have been the playground of some race of giants in ancient days who left these fantastic building bricks behind them. Occasionally one came upon splendid stretches of veld, of every shade of green, ringed round with hills of the deepest, most exquisite blue. I have never seen such blue in a landscape. Above all are the heavy clouds of the rainy season, great bulging grey udders, swelling with moisture and ready at any moment to burst and to descend, not in a sprinkle but in a solid rush of water. Such a cloud-burst was a contributary cause to the troubles which now faced us, though two great rivers, the Pungwe and the Zambesi, are both said to have overflowed their banks.

Everything now depended upon the weather keeping fine, but my heart sank rather when I rose in the middle of the night, stood on the rear platform of the train and found that it was pouring and that 3 inches had been registered in two hours. About seven o'clock in the morning the sky cleared and we entered the terrible Pungwe Marshes, a place which Dante might have made one of his Circles in hell. For hundreds of square miles, when the waters are out, there is a horrible morass, a primitive chaos of slime, weeds and oozing dark brown water in which every vile creature which crawls or flies and can shoot venom into man finds its home. Mosquitoes buzzed round us and poisonous flies and hornets shot through the windows, while if we closed them the humid heat became more than one could stand. It was a nightmare place, reeking with putrescence. Along a very narrow sandy bank the train gingerly crept, and it was clear, as one looked at the fissured sides, that they had been badly shaken by the floods and might give way under the weight. As we were in the first train to pass, it was purely experimental, and no one could tell what would happen. One side slip and the carriage would have reeled down into that awful marsh, giving us a peculiarly slow and unpleasant exit, which would have furnished a text no doubt for some of our more bitter clerical opponents. However, by crawling along we made our way onwards until we came to a place which was too dangerous to pass. Here we were all turned out, and as we tramped along the line to meet the rescue train which we could see in the far distance we met the long drove of the passengers from Beira three days over-due who were making their way to the train which we had just quitted. Four snakes were accounted for by our party in that short walk. The only redeeming feature of this hellish place, where there is death in the very air, is the bird life, which is very full and varied. There are great cranes everywhere. We saw pelicans in the distance. Coloured kingfishers flitted about, and there was one little red bird, no larger than a wren, which was like a flying flame. No doubt in dry weather the Pungwe Flats may have attractions, but the Lord save us from ever again sampling it in the rains.

Every here and there in the expanse of turbid water one could see little conical straw projections like beehives, which puzzled us much until we realized that they were the tops of submerged kraals of the natives. We were nine hours late at Beira, and very glad we were to find ourselves at last in the quiet of the hotel, our dangerous passage safely accomplished. The weather broke badly immediately afterwards and I believe that we were not only the first but also the last train to win through. Such floods are periodical and there are legends of one some years ago when the water came so suddenly that the natives had to clamber on to the tops of their huts, from which they were lashed by the tails of crocodiles. Why anyone should live in such a place is certainly a mystery.

Beira is a remarkable town. We were told much that was evil before we came, but we did not find this justified. It is true that the Savoy Hotel is rather more expensive than its London namesake, but on the other hand it has verandas which look right out upon the Indian Ocean, and how can one appraise that upon a bill? The streets are broad, and a system of hand-driven trollies makes it easy and pleasant to get about. There is a club and a golf course. No, Beira is not a bad place in spite of the heat and the flies.

One of the pioneer inhabitants, Mr. Tom MacDonald, gave me some particulars. All this Coast is governed, not by Portugal but by a private Company, the Mozambique Company, which is on the lines of the old Chartered Company of Rhodesia, but with more restricted powers. Everything is referred to Lisbon. Mr. MacDonald says – what I have often heard – that when you get a really high-class Portuguese you get one of the finest gentlemen in the world. Such a one is Andrade, who is now Governor. Such men make one understand the wonderful things which Portugal did when at the height of her energy. What enormous driving power there must have been which sent her sons up from this Coast across 500 miles of savage country as far as the gold reefs in Southern Rhodesia! You have to traverse the country, the marshes, the rivers and the mountains, to realize what it meant. But if there is a high-class Portuguese there is also a low one, and some stern remonstrance from Great Britain would not be out of place, as regards the police bullying from which many of our people have suffered in their African ports.

Beira, though it has only a population of 15,000, 2,000 of whom are white, is laid out on a large and ambitious scale, and promises to be a worthy entrance to a great country. It will seem strange, however, to our descendants to think that in this year, 1929, there was no road of any sort connecting the port with Rhodesia. This place is very essential to Rhodesia, and if it were in the market that Dominion should pawn its shirt to buy it; but Portugal is our old and valued ally, and I hope and believe that we will play fair and leave to her always that which was hers before ever a British foot was placed in South Africa. At present the Mozambique Company consists of shareholders, a large proportion of whom are British or German. Its capital is 2½ millions. Thus in fact the Government of the country lies in the hands of a Cosmopolitan Board, though, as I have said, it is severely checked from Lisbon.

I understand that Portugal still owes a considerable War debt to Great Britain. Would it not be possible to make this a basis for a deal by which South Africa and Rhodesia might both obtain the ports which are so necessary for their development?

We seem to have struck a streak of adventure after our

rather prosaic travels. The sky looked dangerous upon the day of embarkation, so we hastened to get aboard the *Karoa*, one of the British India boats trading from Durban to Bombay. To collect thirty-six packages amid pouring rain on a disorganized wharf in the midst of a surging crowd of Arabs and Indians is a feat, but we accomplished it successfully and found ourselves and our belongings upon a steam launch, which performed many strange evolutions before it reached the ship, which was a mile from the shore. I could clearly see a third of the keel of the boat behind us, so I could guess that we also presented a lively spectacle to the onlookers. We were hardly aboard, however, before the wind freshened into a gale, and then, as night fell, it developed into a cyclone of unusual power. The harbour is a natural one, ringed round with islands, which, however, have many gaps between. With great skill our captain was able to manoeuvre the *Karoa* and anchor her in the lee of a good shelter, so that we had no sea to contend with. But the wind was terrific, and the rain lashed with such violence that one could not turn one's face to it. Worse and worse it got until it reached a pitch which I can only once equal in my long experience of ocean travel. It was such a typhoon as only a Conrad could describe. As I lay in my bunk at night I expected every hour to hear the thud-bump which would tell me that our anchor had dragged, and that we had drifted on

to the mud banks. Captain Bannehr had steam up, however, and kept easing the strain upon the cable. In the
morning it was clear that my fears had not been in vain,
for three large steamers close beside us were all ashore,
including the pilot boat. The *Malda*, which brought out
the Prince, got adrift in the middle of the night, and
drifted stem foremost down the harbour, hooting wildly
until she reached the mud. Sailors take their risks easily,
but it would be hard to conceive a more nerve-shattering
situation for the *Malda* herself, and for other ships,
including our own, for this heavy battering ram would
have smashed anything which she encountered. By good
luck or good seamanship she got through without accident save to herself, and I see her now through the
porthole with a whole seascape visible under her bows
and forward keel. The situation was very like that which
occurred in Apia Harbour in Samoa some forty years
ago, when the *Calliope* steamed successfully against the
gale, even as we did, and five men-of-war, American and
German, dragged anchor and drifted, with dreadful loss
of life, upon the leeward reefs. The captain tells me that
this was the most severe cyclone of his experience. We
are held up now for a further twenty-four hours,
because the buoys which mark the passage have all been
disarranged. All fresh information shows that the storm
was a real typhoon and that the situation was more
serious than we had supposed. "It was really perilous,

but good seamanship saved the day." So says the *East African Standard*.

Out in the Indian Ocean. Heavy grey clouds on every side. I hope that more trouble is not brewing. However, we have a stout little ship with a most reassuring beam to her. The captain, too, is a first-class man. He has given me the freedom of the bridge, and I had a chat with him there upon strange monsters of the deep. He was interested at my account of the strange marine creature which I saw once in Grecian waters, which made me think that prehistoric monsters might not be so prehistoric after all. He had himself a strange adventure once. His ship slowed down for no discoverable cause. At last he found that his bows had hit a huge ray, which must have been sleeping on or near the surface. It had wrapped itself round the forefoot, and the ship had to be stopped and backed before they could get rid of it. It was as large as the carpet of a good-sized room.

This ship has a crew of Hindoo seamen, whereas the usual Lascars are Mohammedan. A great difference in character was shown by the two in the War. No persuasion could make the Hindoos go west of Suez. On the other hand the Mohammedans made light of danger, went everywhere, and formed the crews of many torpedoed ships. I am glad to say that they have erected a fine monument to these men in India. But it is just that difference between the Hindoo and the Mohammedan which would make the latter the master of India should we leave it.

There is a Mr. Harger on board, a well-known mining geologist, who was the first man to discover the Lichtenburg diamond fields, having located them by a process of severe mental deduction. Like most other people, he is profoundly dissatisfied with the existing diamond laws of South Africa, and yet recognizes the difficulties of the question. He gave me some information about the silver mines of Chicoa, a story which would delight the shade of my friend Rider Haggard. The natives in the Middle Ages used to bring down stores of fine silver to the Portuguese upon the Zambesi, but would never disclose where the mines were. They are marked in a vague way in old Portuguese maps. They were said to be of fabulous richness. That gallant man Colonel Sampson, V.C., led a party to find them, but they entered a village the whole population of which was lying dead from sleeping sickness, which so alarmed his natives that they refused to go on. Since then there has been no serious attempt to find the place. It would be a worthy quest for some adventurous young man.

For two days we have been in the Mozambique Channel, steaming north between the African Coast and Madagascar. I have spent the time in reading carefully and annotating the Gospel of St. John. Often as I have read the New Testament, I never approach it afresh

194

without coming upon something new which I had not observed before. Also as my psychic knowledge grows my appreciation of the Scriptures grows also, for those miracles which used to repel me, as being beyond the bounds of possibility, I know now by my own experience to be well within psychic law. Every detail about Jesus' family life fills me with interest, and though there is not much stated a good deal can be deduced. Since the Scriptures trace Jesus' pedigree, through Joseph to David, it is clear that they admit Joseph to be the father in the ordinary sense, and that the miraculous was an afterthought as seeming to be more honourable. There was a considerable family, at least four brothers and two sisters, and, what I had not before observed, Jesus' brothers discouraged and derided His mission. This is stated in so many words in John vii. 3, 4, 5. Probably His mother disapproved also, which would account for the cold and distant way in which He occasionally addressed her. Of Joseph we know next to nothing, but if he survived he was probably a dissenter, since he is never mentioned as associating with the disciples. All this lends point to His repeated declaration that one had to give up one's own family when one took up such a mission. It also fits in with the record that when He visited His home town of Nazareth He could do no wonders, for the people had little faith. The unfortunate medium who is expected to perform miracles in the presence of acrid critics is in a position to appreciate this passage.

There is a delightfully human touch in the repeated claims in John's Gospel, that he, John, was the beloved Apostle. The other three make no mention of the matter.

I had come aboard the *Karoa* with the firm intention of having a real rest, which I badly needed, but as usual I was asked to speak on the psychic question, and also, as usual, I felt that I was bound to accept. Mr. Sastri, the famous Indian representative and orator, took the chair. Sastri is a Brahmin, and gave an interesting comparison between his own views and mine, when my lecture was over. He said that there was a great analogy. Reincarnation, which is an open question with British Spiritualists, though it is accepted by the Latin races who follow Allen Kardec, was the very corner-stone of the Brahmin system. The successive lives were, however, at long intervals, so that, as it seems to me, the intermediate experience was the more important. Here his views were very unsatisfactory. The soul seemed to be drifting about in a vague way with no particular individuality. Our own knowledge that nothing changes and that practical life in a new environment carries on is infinitely more logical and more satisfying. Sastri admitted many cases of what seemed to be spirit intervention. On the whole the impression left upon my mind was that these people had had a true revelation at some time, but that it had got misunderstood and muddled in the course of time. I have come across passages from the Veddas which seemed to me to be pure spiritualism.

That wretched typhoon at Beira has quite disorganized our programme, and has made us so late that we, being a mail boat and tied by contracts, have to hurry on to make up for lost time. Thus, although we had a fascinating glimpse of Dar-es-Salaam, which was lately the German stronghold of Africa, we were unable to go ashore. It presents a grim reminder of War days, for a huge iron floating dock blocks up part of the entrance to the harbour, a desperate attempt to shut out the inevitable. The town lies up a winding estuary and is a beautiful place, shrouded in palm trees. Will it ever be given back to Germany? No one knows what a mandate may be, or what situation would be created if a majority of the League of Nations were suddenly to announce that the term had expired. Personally I should like to see Germany with some safety-valves. It is dangerous to stifle a nation of 65 million souls. The more you compress them the more you invite an explosion. But the practical difficulties will be immense. All sorts of vested interests are being built up – most of them East Indian. Then again if one mandate goes, what about the others? The whole map of the world would be in the melting-pot once more. But personally I fear lest our Empire outgrow its strength and excite universal enmity because it blocks every one's path. And yet on the moral side I admit that it is a good thing that the Union Jack should spread, and that it is an evil moment for a land when that symbol of civilization is withdrawn. Even the United States, the supreme secession, would have been a far happier and grander land had she found, as with patience she could have found, a constitutional remedy for her grievances, and so become in time the centre of the huge united English-speaking federation.

Zanzibar we saw by night, looking not unlike Venice in the moonlight. There also we could not land, but we noted the great palace of the Sultan, who occupies a position not unlike the protected princes of India. That was our last halt before we came to the long white coral island of Kilindini, which encloses the ancient port of Mombasa, gateway to the Kenya Highlands.

CHAPTER X

A Sporting Colony – The Railway Zoo – The Asiatic Question
– Miss Mayo's Book – A Day's Hunting – Drinking Habits –
Tarlton's Farm – Native Question – Economics – The American
Zola – A Lost Farm – The Man-eater – Psychic Experiences –
John Boyes.

There is something refreshingly breezy and inconsequential about the foundation of the Kenya Colony which appeals greatly to one's sporting instincts. Here are some 12,000 Britons of the very best type stuck up on a high African plateau as far from the sea as London is from Liverpool, and one wonders, as James the First did over the apples in the dumpling, how on earth they got there. When one realizes that at first it was a most lion-haunted area, and that fierce, unconquered tribes of Masai watched the whole strange transaction, it becomes even more remarkable.

To one who views it from outside it would almost seem as if some thirty years ago some high Panjandrum found he had an unexpected surplus of public money and asked a sporting colleague what he should do with it. "Well, what do you say to a railroad?" "Where to?

Well, does it matter? Any old place." "By Jove, a good idea! Where shall we start it?" "Here's an old Portuguese port called Mombasa. What about that?" "Splendid. Where shall we go to?" "Well, there is a lake up yonder, some 500 miles inland. Also there is a place called Uganda, and some day some one may want to come down by train." "So be it. Let us get to it." So the railway was built, mainly by East Indian labour, with occasional pauses while Colonel Paterson or some other sportsman shot off the lions who fed on the Hindoos. Then there came along a fresh lot of freaks – the men with a little money and a taste for adventure. The whole settled and ordered British Empire was open to them, but they must needs come along and sniff the end of this queer railway. "I say, old bean, here's a line. Shall we go up it?" "By all means. You bring your missus and I'll bring mine." So up they went with their families and others came after, and echoes of high romance came back to England, and Winston Churchill wrote it up, and now right in the very heart of black Africa there is this extraordinary wedge of 12,000 samples of our very best, together with a little assortment of excellent Dutchmen and Scandinavians. Don't imagine them to be castaways. Give them their heads, a free hand, and plenty of arms, and they would overrun black Africa as surely as Clive overran India. A mettlesome, high-spirited lot of Britons as ever founded an Empire.

However, I have got rather ahead of my narrative. In the early afternoon of Thursday, February 7th, we bade farewell to Captain Bannehr and his stout little vessel the *Karoa*, and we sampled as much of Mombasa as we could see between the wharf and the station. The port seemed to me to be an amazingly busy and ambitious place, and there is a line of sheds along the waterfront which would not be out of place in Southampton. Cotton, sizal, and coffee seemed to be the chief exports, and I was handed some statistics on the subject. I was handed also something which interested me more – a free pass for self and luggage along the railway. The Governor had also sent an official to welcome us. There was quite a warm glow from Nairobi.

At half-past four we started our journey upon the famous Uganda Railway, which combines the attractions of a Zoo to the usual amenities of travel. We gathered that it was not till morning that we would see the sights, and indeed there was no need for us to rise early, for it is not until the journey is three-quarters completed that one really gets in touch with the wild fauna. There is a huge plain, an immense savannah, with distant blue hills, and at one point far and dim a distant bulk with a white summit. This is Kilimanjaro, the highest peak in Africa, but nearly 100 miles away. Over the great plain one sees on both sides of the line very large herds of buck, of antelopes, and of gnu, with occasional little groups of ostriches. The spacious days are past when rhino horns were picked out of the boilers, and the favourite stamping ground of the Baboo station-master was the top of the water tank, but none the less it would be an unreasonable tourist who did not admit that a trip up this line of railway was a very unique experience.

The first view of Nairobi is not dignified, as it comprises the native quarters, but the town itself gives that young-giant-on-the-make impression which classes it with Salisbury and Bulawayo. Considerable stone buildings alternate with primitive wooden shacks. We were met by several kind friends, one of whom, Mr. Mayer, the proprietor of the *East African Standard*, took us off at once to our hotel, the Norfolk, a comfortable but rather old-fashioned hostel, which proved eventually to be one of the most restful spots which we had found in all our travels. A large modern hotel has been built in the town, but never once did we feel inclined to change our repose for the dust and noise of the main street. The evening was eventful for Malcolm, for a moth which really might have been a swallow came swooping down to our verandah and was cleverly caught by him. He reports it as of the Atlas variety.

I met at Nairobi Mr. Alexander Davis, who is not only a very energetic local citizen who has a share in every enterprise from the local theatre to model farming, but is known honourably in a larger world as the author of

A Layman's Philosophy and other books. He is at present in the "When you are dead you are dead" phase of mental development, so that we had much high argument. He took me out to see his grain fields, which are now nearly ripe, but in imminent danger from the locusts, which are so numerous this year that some native districts are threatened with famine, and the Governor has had to forbid the exportation of foodstuffs. The wheat is of a special type called Kenya Governor, and is remarkable for its hardy growth and its immunity from rust. It is only within the last few years that the Colony has become self-supporting in this matter, but now it has hopes of exporting. It exports maize already in considerable quantities, and Mr. Davis was sending 250 tons over to the London market.

I had become somewhat depressed over the East Indian question, for these picturesque and industrious Asiatics seemed to me to be overrunning the whole East Coast, and leaving very few openings for the European. At Dar-es-Salaam, for example, they had taken advantage of the forced sale of German property and owned much of the town. As I look out of my window as I write I see a small house being erected beside the hotel. A dignified Indian, bearded and turbanned, sits on the unfinished roof, directing the job. Three others are down below with chisels and blocks of stone, tap-tapping from morning to night. Yet another planes out the planks. The stone and the wood are carried by black men. Somewhere in the background there may or may not be a white architect. That seems to summarize the relation of the three races. When the architect also is dark, what remains for the European?

But Mr. Davis is optimistic. The tide has turned, he says. The Briton is the better worker in every phase of life, and has come into his own. The old Indian bazaars which were predominant have been ousted by the European shops. The assistants who were Eastern are now young Britishers. This is as it should be. It would be very dangerous if it were not so. It is to be remembered that this Colony from a military point of view is by no means secure. It is surrounded by black millions. If they rose, it is not certain what view the black soldiers and police would take. In Matabeleland they joined the rebels. If such a situation arose here, everything would depend upon the local Defence Force. This is so far recognized that every white man is conscripted as a trained soldier. But the East Indians are useless. They are not of the fighting races. They would have themselves to be protected, for the blacks love them not. They would be the first victims in a rising. In the German War they were of little or no use. Therefore it would be a dangerous thing if their numbers were to increase out of proportion to the white population. Mr. Davis says that the tide has turned also in Natal, but I did not hear this in Durban.

I have been horrified lately by Miss Mayo's *Mother India*. If her facts are true – and it is well documented – then never has the world seen such organized devil worship as this Brahmin religion. The details given of the necessity for the young girls being married even before they have reached puberty and the physical results are ghastly. The one man I admired was the British member of Council who on being threatened with agitation said that when it was a matter of saving the children his only answer was: "Agitate and be damned." If there be any potency in the Christ's curse upon those who ill-use the children, then it were better for every Brahmin that he have that mill-stone round him and be cast into the sea. There are some details about these child marriages which make one feel that Baboo and baboon may be very near akin. I suppose there are some good men among them – Sastri is a Brahmin – but their system is absolutely diabolical. It is ironic, too, that they should be clamouring for enlarged powers while all the time they are trampling down 60 millions of their fellow-countrymen into the mud, and declaring that they are untouchable. One thing seems to me to be very certain, and that is that if we were to leave India – and I don't think we should be weaker if we did so – after a period of turmoil the whole peninsula would be a great Mahomedan State and these foolish and noisy agitators would be in their graves. The Moplah rising was instructive, for the moment the Mahomedans got on the war trail they destroyed not the British but every Hindoo upon whom they could lay their hands. The survivors went about the country afterwards screaming that Swaraj was their undoing. It is extraordinary that so intelligent a man as Gandhi does not understand so obvious a thing. One of the deepest things in the book was the saying by some scientific authority that the British had sinned against the human race by preserving a stock which without their protection would long ago have been destroyed by the races of the North. It seems a hard saying, but it will bear some thought. This religion among other things makes India the distributing centre for nearly every disease. The world has a right to say a word over that.

It is interesting to know that of the Indians in Africa at least a third were originally of the untouchable class who enjoy a freedom which they could never have had at home. The most beautiful thing in Miss Mayo's book – a passage which can hardly be read without a lump in the throat – is the meeting between the untouchables and the Prince of Wales. I venture to say that it was one of the most truly Christ-like episodes in history. I should add that the poor Indians are rather to be pitied than blamed, since they live under a tyranny more terrible than any earthly ruler could inflict. It is the Brahmin, the priest, who is the villain of the piece and the root of all evil.

To-day, February 12th, we have, through the kind

invitation of Mr. Edgley, enjoyed a day's sport upon his farm, which is situated upon the Athi Plains, about 25 miles from Nairobi. We started, my two boys and I, crammed into a motor, with Mr. Edgley himself, a native skinner and an assortment of firearms. It was not yet six o'clock, and pitch-dark, when we got off, and it was a marvellous thing to see the sun rise on the great steppes which surround the town. We were hardly clear of the outlying buildings before we began to see game in the early morning light. Two large creatures, kongoni, dashed in front of the motor, one of them clearing the road at a single enormous bound. Our host, an experienced sportsman, said that it was the longest jump that he had ever seen a kongoni give. As we drove he told me some of his own varied sporting experiences. The most remarkable was that he had once seen, and actually photographed, a giraffe killing a lion. The great creature protecting its young had reared up and had brought its fore-feet down with a crash upon the lion's skull, shattering it to pieces.

After an hour and a half of rather rough driving we arrived at the farm, where we were met by Major Dunman, one of the pioneers of the Colony, and a famous sportsman. Like most good sportsmen he had shown himself to be a fine soldier on occasion, and had distinguished himself in the War. I found that he, together with other Kenyans, had a very great respect for the German General in command, while their admiration for our own Commanders, save only Smuts, was more moderate.

A second motor-car was waiting, and having divided ourselves into a rifle party and a shot-gun party we set out in search of adventures. I belonged to the latter, in spite of which I managed to get a small antelope of a rare variety. Its death, I'm glad to say, was instantaneous. When we met at lunch we found that each of the boys had been successful, Denis getting a kongoni and Malcolm a kongoni and a Thompson's gazelle. It is really shooting for the pot, since every morsel is devoured. A wildebeest was partially eaten by a lion, but we did not get a glimpse of his majesty himself. Many herds of zebras trotted about in the distance, and there were numerous ostriches. At one point we came upon eight giraffes, one of them an enormous creature. I had my cinema-camera with me, and with this I took about 50 feet of reel, with what luck only the future can show. At another spot we came upon a dead gazelle with three huge vultures rending and riving its body. A white-headed eagle sat moodily by, on the top of an antheap, awaiting its turn. This is a usual comradeship, and the party is often completed by a marabout stork, a sort of master of ceremony in black tail coat and white waistcoat, who does not eat much himself but presides at the banquet like some benevolent old uncle.

In the one morning we had seen a very fair variety of the fauna of the country – mostly at close quarters. There had been buck of at least four species, hartebeeste, gnus, giraffes, zebras, ostriches, warthogs, and many kinds of birds. As we returned we added locusts to our list, as a swarm came drifting past and into the car, exactly like a snowstorm. We reached our comfortable Norfolk Hotel in the late afternoon after one of the most pleasant days of all our travels.

Some curious points arise in talking to these experienced old hunters. One of them is that game is not usually afraid of lions – or possibly that they know exactly when a lion means mischief and when he is surfeited and therefore harmless. They describe how they have seen lions walking past or through the herds which go on grazing with unconcern. On the other hand the leopard is a creature which kills for the sake of killing – a bad sportsman among animals – and the weaker creatures fly at his approach.

I remember that when I was captain of our home golf club a young professional asked me what sort of place Nairobi was, as he had had the offer of a billet on the course there. I answered that it was the sort of place where he might meet a lion at the ninth hole. When I recounted this small jest here I was assured that it was literally true, and that lions did occasionally penetrate into the very suburbs of the town. A year or so ago they became so numerous, on account of the game preserves, that Mr. J.A. Hunter was specially told off to thin them down, and he got eighty-four in a very short time, as well as ten leopards. These things also will some day seem like an incredible legend.

I made some inquiry here about the Missionary question, and I am sorry to say that the reports from grave and responsible men were exactly as I had them in Rhodesia. It is impossible for me to doubt any longer in the face of the testimony that the Mission boys – or those at least who find their way into the world – are below the standard of the raw natives in all the essential virtues.

My informants were certainly not prejudiced, for one of them recounted with great appreciation the conduct of two young Mission boys upon a special occasion. But they are the more impertinent, the more dishonest and the more immoral. I asked whether this applied to Roman Catholic as well as Protestant Missions and the answer was that it did. The worst, however, appeared to be the American Missions with their four-square evangelical dogmas and their hobnobbing with the blacks. One apparently trustworthy witness told me how he had seen a female missioner (non-British), of not too mature an age, kiss all the black adult boys who had assembled upon the platform to meet her train. The witness said that the sight made him physically sick, and certainly from the expression of his face I thought that the mere memory of it was about to have the same effect. I put forward Mr. Glossop's appeal as to the moral police, but it was met with derisive laughter. And yet Livingstone and Moffat did great work in their day, and so too did the Jesuit Fathers on the Red Indian Mission. But it was the presence of civilized man, and the gentle atmosphere of Christianity, and not the often nonsensical dogmas, which prevailed. The subject leaves one sad, for there can be no question of the good intention and self-sacrifice of many of these people – nor, I fear, of their complete failure. The order of merit of the various bodies varies, but the general lay opinion puts the Roman Catholic first, as teaching practical trades, the Scottish second, and all agree that the American is the last. They also agree that a decent Mahomedan is far ahead either of the raw native or of the Mission boy in everything which makes a man. Mahomet wrought a great work in Africa.

I see that Sir Arthur Davies has been discussing in the Press the drinking habits of this Colony. There are certainly some very hard drinkers among the Colonists, and it is a thousand pities in a land which calls for every effort upon the part of its inhabitants. The indictment applies, however, to a floating minority of the population who may catch the eye on account of the unusual nature of their lives but who do not represent the average hard-working and decent settler. Still I think that Sir Arthur Davies did a good service to Kenya by calling attention to the matter, and if it might do any good I would gladly second his attempt to clean this reproach away from a splendid group of British people. There is no doubt that a certain proportion, both men and women, do degenerate here, and become failures owing to drink, and therefore it would be well that public opinion should be aroused on the point, and that the cocktail, the sundowner and the old-fashioned "have a drink" idea, which has greatly died out in England, may receive a check. I fancy, however, that the matter is better than it was, but there is plenty of room for a crusade in favour of temperance. This I say not as an unfriendly critic, but as one who is peculiarly interested in the welfare of so fine a Colony. But I am sure that it is a passing phase and that all will be well. The chief offenders are often to be found among the casual visitors rather than the Kenyites.

We had a wonderful experience upon February 14th, when Mr. Henry Tarlton took us out to his game preserve, where no shooting is allowed, save the many shots which I took with my camera. Though it is only 6 miles from the town, this estate, which covers 10,000 acres of broken and varied country, is swarming with all sorts of wild creatures. My wife, Billy and I made up the party, and with Tarlton driving us we careered wildly over the vast plain, flying down declivities and up slopes in a way which should have qualified us as dirt-track experts. The whole savannah was studded with groups of animals, and in many cases they allowed us to come quite close before they took alarm. There were great droves of the beautiful little Thompson's gazelles, tawny brown striped with white. Then there were the larger kongonis, many of them finely antlered and the size of small cows. A drove of wild boars and warthogs scuttled past us, and then we saw the finest sight of all, a herd of zebras, a hundred or more strong, who galloped past, their hooves drumming, their manes streaming, their heads tossing, the very embodiment of glorious and tumultuous life. A number of large elands were embedded among them and joined in their frantic stampede. One water-buck, a big grey sad-eyed creature, allowed me to approach within 20 yards of him. Ostriches abounded. Some poacher has been putting in his murderous work, for in four separate places we found vultures scrabbling over the carcasses of buffaloes, which had bullet marks upon their hides.[1] Tarlton is a small man, but he has a grim face and is dangerous when angered. He loves his animals, and I should have pitied the poachers if they had fallen into his hands. Once we thought we saw the movement of a lion among some bushes, but we were

---

[1] This proved to be a mistake. They had died of disease.

unable to put him up, though his little pal the jackal was much in evidence. Altogether it was an unforgettable day, and as we came back, heading towards a strange blood-red sun which shone through a cloud bank, we marvelled over the beauty and wonder of Nature.

Tarlton, who is a famous heavy-game shot, second only to his famous brother, told me one curious observation about vultures. In each group he says there is one chief. When a circle is formed round the prey, this loathsome chief hops forward and devours the two eyes. Then he stands aside and his subjects all rush in.

To turn from the particular to the general, this country, like all our African possessions, is deeply concerned over the native question, which is so urgent and important that some think that it may even split the Empire in two. It might be briefly stated thus, so far as I can follow what even the Colonists admit to be very complex. There is a native State named Buganda which has for centuries had a government of its own, with king, council, officers, taxes, and all the details of a going concern. And it worked. It has therefore been taken as the type for tribal management, not only in Uganda, to which it belongs, but also in Tanganyika, and to some extent here in Kenya, where the Masai have their own self-governed reserve. On the other hand there have been very many broken clans, as the Scots would say – that is detribalized natives who have no natural rulers. These constitute a problem. It is all very well for distant officials to draw up regulations, but the Colonists are brought in daily contact with these people, and it is impossible for them to bring in their crops or run their estates without native labour. If the native is treated so generously that he already has in his reserves everything which he could possibly want, then why should he ever hire himself out to help the white man? The Colonists, or many of them, feel that life here would become impossible if all legislation was in favour of the native – which they claim to be the case. When one hears them describe their difficulties one cannot help feeling in sympathy, and one is sorry too for Sir Duncan Cameron of Tanganyika or the Governor here, who has to obey orders from home and carry out a policy which is unpopular with those among whom he has to dwell.

The great Athi Plains lie to the south of the town – those plains upon which we had our day of safari. By the way, upon that day a wandering rhinoceros was seen crossing Mr. Edgley's farm, and we should certainly have looked rather foolish if with our shotguns we had come across him. To-day we explored the foothills to the north of the town, where we visited Mr. Edgley's hill farm, and saw at 7,000 feet all the familiar English flowers in full bloom. It was indeed a glimpse of fairyland. In the evening we returned by another route which took us through the coffee lands, which look most prosperous and are not affected by locusts, several swarms of which came drifting up to and into the car. The price of good coffee land is from £10 to £20 an acre, and it takes four years before they bear. After that a friend of mine found that he could make an average net profit of £11 per acre from his coffee. The ordinary cotton lands of the plain varies from £1 to £3 per acre. There is really nothing which cannot be grown in this wonderful soil and climate. Coffee, tea, sugar, sizal, cotton, almonds, tobacco – I think that cocoa and rubber were the only commodities that I could not trace.

A curious point about coffee, which would have interested Monsieur Fabre, is that its worst enemy is a small creature called the mealy bug. It is found that this pest is carried there by ants, who place it upon the berry, and then suck the sweet juice which is exuded by the bug. Creosote rags are tied round the stems to keep the creatures from climbing up with their living burdens, and this is the only device by which they can be stopped.

I have been agreeably occupied in reading Upton Sinclair's *Boston*. I look upon Sinclair as one of the greatest novelists in the world, the Zola of America, and his power of detail and of marshalling facts leaves me amazed. I think he has become almost monomaniacal in his reaction against our settled law and order, but his high, unselfish soul shines through it all, and if half of what he says is true – and it is well documented – then Sacco and Vanzetti, the two anarchists, were undoubtedly put to death unjustly by the State of Massachusetts. Police procedure and judicial procedure and the whole criminal administration of the United States would seem now to be among the worst in the world, and torture is often as much a part of that system as it was in mediæval Italy, though disguised under a specious name. We have little right to criticize, for the shame of Glasgow over the Slater-Trench scandal is quite as great as that of any American frame-up; but two blacks do not make a white, and if one has protested against the one, one may be allowed to do so against the other.

It is impossible to read the facts without realizing that the two Italians were executed not as murderers but as anarchists. On the other hand it might fairly be argued that as an anarchist is a man who is admittedly out to destroy the State, the State has an equal right to destroy him. Even if this were so, however, it should not be done under the pretence that the man is an ordinary vulgar criminal. Far from this being the case Vanzetti was a man of such rare and exalted character, in spite of his extreme social views, that one thinks of St. Francis of Assisi as one reads his utterances. His personality is likely to grow into a legend. As to his possible participation in the crime, the evidence became so complex that the public could not see the true proportion of the various pleas. I would take one as being in itself final. On the morning of the murder he was shown by a whole string of witnesses to have been selling eels many miles from the scene of the crime. These witnesses were supposed by the defence to be all in conspiracy to shield the prisoner. Late in the proceedings the defence had the idea to approach the wholesale eel merchants. Seven years had elapsed, but by some miracle the dusty old invoice had been preserved and it was shown that on the day before they had actually forwarded a barrel of eels to Vanzetti. Surely that alone should be enough for any reasonable man.

Last night I gave my first lecture to a crowded theatre with a sporting audience who sent up an excellent lot of questions. Denis at my request stood up bravely and gave his own experience, which impressed the people deeply. Altogether it was a very successful evening, and I have given the good people of Kenya something to ponder and discuss. I am always amazed at the way in which fresh and unspoiled minds can follow the psychic argument, while worldly-wise and sophisticated ones go astray. A supreme example is Bernard Shaw, whose recent interview upon the subject has just been forwarded to me from England. His argument is that he himself has cheated at the séance table and has successfully deceived trusting friends, and that therefore all phenomena are suspect and worthless. To put this argument into concrete form, I have in the presence of witnesses unquestionably seen my mother since her death. But what I say must be false because Bernard Shaw cheated his friends. Was there ever a more absurd *non sequitur* than that? And yet it is gravely put forward by one of the cleverest men of the age. *Exaltavit humiles.* The photographic lecture has also been a success. I had only one interruption. It was when I was showing the psychic conditions when Elias and Moses were materialized on the mountain. "But neither of them had ever died," cried a voice in the audience. There is an orthodoxy which is surely very near to lunacy. I could only answer that everyone was welcome to his own ideas, but that the general opinion was that these people had been dead some time.

To-day, February 23rd, has been notable for another of those excursions which for all of us will make our memories of Nairobi like glimpses of some other world. Mr. Edgley, who has shown us great consideration and kindness, had purchased or been given or won in a raffle a farm which lay in such entirely ungetatable country that he had only three times in his life approached it. He simply let it lie fallow as a place where game might wander and where some Masai caretaker could feed his cattle. He had the happy inspiration now to go and look at his neglected acres, and we three males went with him. It was a case once more of a start in the darkness, of the faint flush of dawn stealing over the eastern sky and shedding an opalescent beauty over the great Athi Plain. For 10 miles or so we kept to rough cart-tracks, which connected up scattered farms, and then finally even those died away, and we were out in the blue with nothing but the great expanse of withered grass before us, stretching, an old-gold wilderness, to the far horizon. Sometimes the veld was smooth and we made good progress. Sometimes we got among outcrops of rock and had to go back or steer round. At one time we found ourselves on a plain dotted with trees – acacias, I believe. "Good lord, look at that!" cried Edgley. There, close to us, was a huge giraffe nibbling the leaves from the top of one of the acacias. Near it was another and yet another – seven in all. With luck I have collected them in my cinema camera, and I may yet see the huge beasts doing their lurching canter across my music-room wall.[1] We were now lost and had to inquire at a native kraal, the inhabitants of which are so primitive that on occasion they are suspected of cannibalism. They looked at the car with big white eyeballs projecting from their brutish faces, and no persuasion could get one to guide us. We saw, however, soon afterwards a winding line of green among the yellow savannah, and knew that it marked the course of the Athi River, which was one of

[1] I have done so.

220

our landmarks. It was comical to see our host standing up with his hand shading his eyes, and muttering, "Now where the devil is that house of mine? I certainly had a house somewhere here." At last we struck the river, which was now only a series of sombre tree-shaded pools, dark olive in colour, with dried mud between. Then we rested, as the servants could bring what was wanted from the deserted hut. The same servants had urgent news. There were two man-eating crocodiles of immense size in the river; one had taken a full-sized bullock the night before, and also a native child within the last week. Denis and Malcolm set off at once with rifles, and an excited Masai arrived presently to tell us that the worst of the two monsters had been slain. When Edgley and I arrived we found an excited group on the banks of the river. It seems that Malcolm had seen the brute's head projecting from the water and had fired, at intervals, six bullets into it, the creature rearing out of the water, gnashing its huge jaws and beating the stagnant pool into foam. It had now sunk dead to the bottom, not more than six paces from the bank, where it could be touched with a long rod. Our only certainty as to its death lay in the fact that no bubbles came up, and we were aware of course that its mate was in hiding close by, in spite of which with great hardihood the two boys partly stripped and plunged in nearly up to their waists, aided by a young English chauffeur who drove the spare car. A bribe of 20s. failed to move any of the natives to help. The boys got the tail above the surface, but the brute was so large that it was impossible to move him, and I was so convinced that the situation was dangerous that I called them all in. Even then our difficulties were not over, for the bank was so steep and slippery that they only clambered up by using my feet and legs as a ladder, while I held on to prevent my being pulled in. It was a sore disappointment to Malcolm that he should not have the specimen, but the chief native promised that in two days the body would rise, when he would bring the head and skin into Nairobi. This he duly did.

That native chief opened my eyes. He was a naked savage, but his herd, which I saw, numbered 400, which at the current rate meant £4,000 worth of property, apart from many other items. When our people subscribe for the poor natives I wonder if they realize how often they are affluent men. This man never sold a bullock and used them only for buying wives – ten bullocks being the price. He sold his female children at the same rate, and it was all pure business. I remember old General Drayson, the great astronomer, telling me how he lived among the Zulus in early days, and how when they watched him courting an English girl they expressed disgust, and said, "Why does he not pay his cows like a man!"

That was, our chief adventure of the day, but on our

return journey Malcolm got two Thompson's gazelles, the second being a very brilliant shot. These were a welcome addition to our larder, though Malcolm himself, being a vegetarian, would profit little. We lost our way as before, but finally, weary, but full of wonderful memories, we made our way into Nairobi.

It is amazing how these cars stand the rough driving on the veld. They are nearly all American, and the same holds good of South Africa, but not of Rhodesia, where the splendid patriotism of the people gives an unwritten preference to British goods. It is a pity that our manufacturers have not met the need, though I hear they are improving. What is wanted is a rough strong chassis, heavily engined – say 20 h.p. – so that one has not to change gear at every slope, and with the body slung high so as to give lots of room for stones and inequalities. Provide all this for £200, and the market is waiting.

I am much struck by the account of the experiences of Count Centurione Scotto in the castle of Millesimo near Genoa. Consider the bald facts. The Count belongs to one of the oldest families in Italy. He lost his son. He read Bradley's account of his own experiences with the medium Valiantine. He set out for London and joined the Bradley circle. He got messages in Italian which he was convinced came from his son. He found that one of the Bradley spirit controls was an Italian peasant, D'Angelo. He asked the spirit D'Angelo if he would come back to Italy and help to make a circle there. D'Angelo said he would. The Count returned to his castle, formed a circle of high-class people, which eventually included the well-known Professor Bozzano, and, lo! all the spirit controls of the Bradley circle came through with the direct voice, D'Angelo dominating the circle. Bradley was not there – Valiantine was not there. And yet here were the whole phenomena reproduced with numerous apports brought through walls, and other wonders. How can any reasonable man – I do not consider the fumblers who occasionally call themselves psychic researchers to be "reasonable men" – doubt such evidence as that? And it reacts on all the past. Are there any words which human speech can use which are adequate for the apology which is due to the early pioneers of Spiritualism?

But to me, in spite of the messages from Napoleon, Rabelais, and other famous men, the most interesting of all was that to the Roman Catholic Church. It was started by Victor Hugo, but it was strengthened by a spirit who was clearly the late Pope, who was said in his lifetime to have strong mediumistic powers. The message was for the Vatican, and it was to the effect that the Spiritualistic movement was all in the interest of religion and that it was "an urgent necessity in the best interests of the Catholic Church not to let other Christian sects outstrip them in studying and assimilating present-day evidences of survival." The matter seems to me to be of great importance, and those interested will find the account in the January number of *Psychic Science*.

I had the interesting experience to-day of meeting John Boyes, who wrote the book *King of the Kikuyu*, recounting his own adventures when by sheer audacity and force of character he pacified and ruled over that savage tribe, risking his life many times in the course of the episode. He gained command over these fierce people at a time when their friendship and co-operation were most necessary for feeding and protecting the workers on the Uganda Railway. No one can read his book without realizing that his influence was certainly to the good, and greatly to the interests of the Empire. He seems to have been scandalously treated by the officials of that time – from 1900 onwards. Perhaps it is not too late even now for the State to bestow upon him some recognition for his wonderful work.

CHAPTER XI

We start for the Great Lake – The Rift Valley – A Dangerous Road – The Gulf of Kavirondo – *Darkened Rooms* – Tanganyika – The Mwanza Jail – The Bishops – Native Football – The Source of the Nile – A Cloud.

To-day, February 26th, we start upon our great adventure, which is to go round Lake Victoria Nyanza in one of the small steamers which ply along the coasts. There are two ways of getting to the Lake, by train or by motor-car. The former is cheap and comfortable. The latter is very dear and entails a most trying journey of over 230 miles of elementary roads. With the perversity of Britons we all voted for the latter.

This involved our spending the night at the half-way town of Nakuru. The journey from Nairobi to Nakuru is monotonous in its early stages, though it is pleasant to see the many good, well-cared-for farms. Then one runs into the native reserve of the Kikuyu, and for 30 miles or so the country is wild. Once a large baboon crossed our road, and once a little herd of impala buck; but otherwise it was uneventful until we came to the escarpment of the Rift Valley, and looked down at that wonderful scene. The valley, which was explored and named by Professor Gregory, is part of a great scar or weal which lies across the face of the world, starting up in the Dead Sea and reaching across Africa to the latitude of Madagascar. It is over 50 miles across, a monstrous groove, with many volcanic traces to point to its origin. As it rises in the place of the dead cities, where the rumour of great destruction still prevails, one wonders whether the whole cataclysm which produced it may not have been the same the legend of which is found in our Scriptures.

It was certainly some tremendous cause which produced such a result. Looking down from the eastern lip an enormous furrow is apparent, held in by mountains, with a vast plain studded with trees at the bottom. One descends by a Class Z road for some 2,000 feet, and then continues one's journey up the plain, passing signs of volcanic activity upon every side. There is one sinister hill, Longanot, with a 3-mile crater, upon the left, which is viewed with horror by the natives, who will not approach its gnarled and channelled sides after dark. They say that the game avoid it too. This also may be a reminiscence of some terrible disaster. One passes several considerable lakes much impregnated with natron, in spite of which the boys were able to distinguish two distant dark spots, the heads of hippopotami, appearing above the surface. If pickle is a preservative, they should live for ever. A rock stands by the wayside where a white trader was killed by the Masai many years ago. Every Masai who passed used to put a pebble on the rock, and the heap of them was plainly visible, though whether this meant approbation of the deed, or whether it was an offering to the spirit of the dead man, was more than we could discover. Some zebras in the distance, and a dignified secretary bird which strutted along the road, completed the sights of interest. To-night we sleep in a snug little bungalow attached to the Nakuru Hotel, where every comfort can be found for the weary traveller. It is strange how often one finds, in such places, all that is wanting in the pretentious city hotel.

In the morning we surveyed from a distance the Nakuru Lake, which is one of many which lie in the gut of the Rift Valley. All these lakes are impregnated with salt, which links them up with the Dead Sea, and the legend of the pillar of salt, all concerned with this great slash in the world's face. The seismic cause of it is accentuated by the fact that one of the largest craters in the world, Menangai, is to be found behind the Nakuru Hotel.

Our drive of 120 miles upon the second day was not all easy going. We took a short cut which runs over the mountains and saves 70 miles as compared with the main road which goes through Eldoret. Few people hazard themselves or their cars in such a journey, but our time was limited, so we chanced it. In parts the road was fair, but there was one long mountain stretch, the best of which was a cart-track and the worst not far off the bed of a river. Our driver was an experienced man, and the boys took turn about to drive the luggage car, relieving the capable young mechanic. There were places on the mountain where a skid would have sent us down the side, and many places where another car, coming the other way, would have presented an impossible problem, for there was no room to pass, and to back on a narrow rocky path for half a mile or so on a steep slope would have tried any driver. Much of the land over which we passed was native reserve, and we were conscious occasionally of a by no means friendly atmosphere. Women grimaced at us and men once or twice glared. Several were carrying spears. On the whole, however, they seemed a harmless and good-humoured crowd.

The land which was open to Europeans seemed to me to be well cultivated. Indeed, I was more impressed by the evidences of permanent settlement in Kenya than I was in Rhodesia, where the great veld seems so unbroken. Here, apart from the game preserves and the native districts, one sees an endless succession of coffee, sizal, sugar and tea plantations, with many houses each in its grove of trees.

The scenery during the day was magnificent and on

the most mighty scale. I cannot remember anything finer. We saw little, however, of the wildlife of the country. A Duiker deer, not larger than an Airedale terrier, ran before us. Among birds I noticed the coraan or lesser bustard, the big black red-beaked bustard, and many varieties of stork and of hawk. In the Vegetable Kingdom the most striking objects were the weird euphorbia, out of which the natives distil poison, and the cork tree with no leaves, and flowers of sealing-wax red shaped like bottle cleaners. The sausage tree, with a whole larder of vegetable sausages hanging down, was also new to me.

It was evening before we came quite suddenly upon Kisumu, which lies in an inlet of the lake and is the starting-point for our voyage. There is no hotel and nowhere to sleep except a Dak bungalow, and there in the mosquito-netted verandah I sit while I make these notes. To-morrow early we go aboard.

The Gulf of Kavirondo, at the end of which the little port of Kisumu is situated, is an offshoot from the big lake, though it is in itself a very large sheet of water. It is named from the Kavirondo tribe, who inhabit all this country and who are the natives whom we saw in the later stages of our motor journey. They are complete savages, with hardly any clothing, but the married women are supposed to wear absurd little tufts on their lower spines which give them, especially when they stoop, a comical hen-like appearance. Their villages have been surrounded with palisades and zarebas for defence against the fierce Nandi warriors from the North, but the blessed British Raj has stepped in, and they are safe from molestation, so that the defences have big gaps in them already.

On the morning of February 28th we made our way down to the steamer and presently we were chugging down the gulf. The *Usoga*, as our ship is called, was one of the gallant little flotilla that waged a naval war against the German boats from the Southern ports. It was a most sporting affair, in which each side had to improvise its material. Both here and on Lake Tanganyika the Germans put up a good fight, but in the end they were cleared off the lakes. Captain Marshall of the *Usoga* was in the midst of it all, and gave us some interesting details. I wonder if the facts of the Great War will ever be known, or be mastered by one single brain. The sideshows were often as dramatic and as earnest as the great central battle.

The Gulf was calm, and after passing the narrows, in which a big chocolate-hued hippopotamus was disporting himself, we emerged into the main lake, which has some claim to be the largest in the world. It is 250 miles by 150. As our route runs along the shore we shall never have the feeling of a spacious sea which we felt when traversing Lake Superior. Our first halting-place, Karungu, was reached late at night. I was on the bridge and could realize the responsibility which weighs upon a sailor when, he approaches a coal-black shore which presents no glimmer of light. At last, in response to our frantic siren, the glimmer of a lantern appeared, and finally we were able to locate the tiny wharf and to land the supplies, which were destined for some gold-mine in the hinterland. The next morning, March 1st, found us in Musoma, an exquisite little bay, studded with islands. It is all very restful – indeed, I cannot remember any other occasion when I have been absolutely out of all possible reach of letters, papers, telegrams or even wireless.

I have been reading with mingled feelings the book of my friend Sir Philip Gibbs, *Darkened Rooms*, in which he deals with Spiritualism. It is excellently written and the character-drawing remarkable, but he makes the mistake of drawing only one side of the picture. There have, of course, been fraudulent mediums in the world, though their number has been very greatly exaggerated. If one said that one-tenth were deliberately dishonest one would overstate it. Therefore to draw a picture of Spiritualism where all the mediums are frauds is untrue and also inartistic, as it gives no light and shade. It is as if I drew a picture of a single drunken or debauched priest, and led the reader to think that this was typical of the Catholic Church.

It is curious also, and an evidence of prejudice, that

whereas the opinions of timid psychic researchers are quoted again and again with respect, because they are negative or indecisive, there is not from end to end one word about the great brains and brave hearts who have not feared to say forthright that they have examined this matter and that it is true and good. We hear of Osty and MacDougall, but never a word of Hyslop and Hodgson, Stead and Crookes, Wallace and Barrett, Driesch and Lodge. The rule of the game seems to be that if you stultify yourself by admitting that you can form no opinion, then you are respectable. Or again in this particular book if instead of using the brain that God has given us you take lazy and cowardly refuge in what Mother Church says, regardless of the fact that Mother Church has always been wrong from Galileo to Darwin, then you are respectable. But if after long weighing of evidence and personal testing you form an opinion that the thing is true, and that it is an all-important revelation and the most cogent argument against materialism, then you simply cease to count and drop out of the discussion, since you have had the temerity to gain a definite mental position. All this seems to me to be a most perverse and illogical way of looking at the matter. However, here is beautiful blue Lake Victoria stretching out on every side of me. God can take care of His own.

We spent the whole of Friday, March 1st, coasting down the Tanganyika shore, which bristles with those curious rock formations which are so characteristic of Africa. There were considerable stretches which seemed to be well cultivated, and we saw continually the kraals of the natives, who have a large reserve. We are a curious little family on board – a high officer of police returning from inspection, the white master of a native school with his wife, a fine young German with Frau and baby, three Greek girls, and one or two nondescripts. The police inspector is quite hopeful about the future of the Colony, and approves of the Home Rule policy of Sir Donald Cameron by which the various tribes rule themselves. He is quite confident that our mandate is a permanent one. Late at night we came into Mwanza at the south end of the lake, a palm-tree-fringed bay, where we have to stay three days in order to connect up with some train from Dar-es-Salaam.

There is some danger that these native tribes will increase beyond all bounds or reason now that Nature's checks are removed. All over the world war exists between Nature and the British Raj. Nature sends smallpox. The Raj sends vaccine. Nature sends the flood. The Raj sends the dam. Nature sends the famine. The Raj supplies the food. Nature sends the bellicose spirit of tribal warfare. The Raj, in the person of the Police Inspector, suppresses it. It has been a long uphill game, but the Raj usually wins. It is the greatest force for good in this world.

Our enforced three days' delay at Mwanza has not been a very exhilarating experience. Even a beautiful island-studded bay and groves of palm trees pall when one is confined to a small boat. It is true that the land lies open to us, and the rest of the family did take a drive round in a crazy car driven by an Indian, who set the boys' teeth on edge every time he changed gear. For my own part I stayed on board nearly all the time, writing or reading. I had one interesting experience, for by the kindness of Mr. Noah, Governor of the jail, I was allowed to go over it and see the prisoners. Mr. Noah had certainly some curious animals in his ark. There were no whites or Indians – all were negroes. Five of these poor devils had conceived the idea that if they were blind they would be liberated, and by rubbing lime, scraped from the walls, into their eyes, they had actually destroyed the sight. They were now engaged in basket plaiting, which they did as well without as with their eyes. But what a craving for their open life of the plain and the forest must have filled the breasts of these men before they did so terrible a deed, and how bitter must have been the blow when they realized that it was all in vain. I read dumb despair upon their uncouth faces. And yet they are very well treated, and there are many prisons at home which are far below the level of this one in cubic space and general comfort. There is very little punishment – only four floggings last year. The intelligent men were being taught trades and I saw articles of furniture made by them. The Missions might perhaps learn something from this method of taming the savage.

I also went over the lunatic cells. One poor little distorted negro seemed to think that he was at a native dance and never ceased advancing and retreating, bowing and kneeling. Another was sunk in deep apathy and never moved. His soul had really left his body and he was but an inert mass with some rudiments of animal life. So motionless was he that after he had eaten or been fed in the yard the birds would settle upon him and pick the crumbs from his thick lips. Both these cases, perfectly hopeless from an orthodox point of view, might, I think, be cured by Dr. Wickland or Dr. Titus Bull on their theory of demonic obsession. Alienists would be wise to give attention to the results which these two doctors have achieved, and they may learn that the Christ was not mistaken in His pathology.

From Mwanza, which none of us ever wish to see again, we jogged on by short stages to Bukoba, Bukakata, etc. Our little company on board had been reinforced by no less than three Roman Catholic bishops who were assembling to confer with a special legate from Rome, Bishop Hinslip of the English College, who has been sent out upon some question of native education. They all seemed very pleasant fellows, though I have no doubt that a few centuries ago they would have gladly made an *auto-da-fé* of myself and every Spiritualist. As it was, I enjoyed several interesting conversations with them. Of the four one was English, one a Swiss, one a Dutchman and one an Alsatian – typical of this wonderful Church. At five in the morning I was on deck, and seeing a light in the saloon, I looked in. The Englishman was saying Mass and the other three were kneeling behind him, all with looks of wrapt devotion upon their faces. It was an impressive sight. What a beautiful religion it would be if it could assimilate Spiritualism, and at the same time get rid of that straitjacket of bigotry and dogma which encompasses it. Perhaps the future of religion lies that way.

These little lake ports are very much like each other, and the voyage becomes rather monotonous. The constant shouting and whirring of the steam winch as cargo is handled, together with the discomfort of wet decks in a very small vessel, make it a little trying for travellers. A few incidents alleviated the dullness of the days. One was the appearance of a large hippo walking up and down the beach close to where the vessel was moored. I did not see the creature, but Denis was called – it was in the early morning – and reported that it was only 50 yards from the ship and looked extraordinary in the glare of a powerful torch. We had a welcome break at Port Bell, whence we ran up by motor to Kampala, which is the capital of Uganda. The boys motored there from Entebbe with a friend. It promises to rival Nairobi in size and importance, and is already embellished by two enormous cathedrals of the rival faiths, and also by the palace of the nominal King. I was most interested by an Association Football match played by two teams of natives. Their form was excellent, and either of them would have given a game to any British team which was short of first class. The combination was perfect, the shooting was good, and I saw a corner kick land in the goal mouth and the ball put through by a woolly head as neatly as any man could wish. It was extraordinary how with his naked foot the goalkeeper could kick the ball a distance which even with a boot would seem remarkable. I think that playing unshod gave the players a quickness and elasticity which made it a very fast game.

The soil of Uganda seems to be extraordinarily rich and the people prosperous, but for some reason which I failed to understand it has not attracted settlers in the same way as Kenya. It may be that the climate is more tropical. Whatever the reason may be, the white men seemed to be nearly all officials, and though we heard about coffee planters and cotton estates we gathered that they were not numerous. The negroes, however, here and all round the lake cultivate coffee of a low grade, and many of them are quite well-to-do, which does not improve their manners or deportment. On the other hand the real negro workers are splendid fellows, and I have never seen men put their whole energy into their labour to the same extent as some of the stevedores handling cargoes upon this lake.

At Jinja we landed to see the Ripon Falls and the source of the Nile. The Nile, or this particular branch of it, flows out of the lake in a stream which is already some 200 yards across, so it is a very lusty infant. It was curious to think, as we watched the rushing stream, that had we dropped a note into it, duly enclosed in a calabash, it would, bar reeds or mud or other accidents, find its way in time via Lake Albert to Cairo and the Mediterranean. The boys got away on their own and saw and fired at several crocodiles and hippos. By some mischance whenever hippos have appeared my wife has missed them, so that I feel I must take her to the Zoo when we return and convince her that such an animal does exist.

A Barney Barnato story was told me by a Uganda gentleman who was intimate with that strange man in early days in Kimberley. It seems that Barnato had a partner with whom he had a most bitter quarrel. If the facts were as narrated, then the partner certainly had cause to be furious. In the heat of his passion he swore that when he died he would see that Barnato died also. My informant, a level-headed man and a lawyer, said that he had heard the man repeat the threat again and again. Years afterwards the man did die, and at that selfsame day and hour Barnato jumped overboard from the ship in which he was returning to England. If this were a coincidence it must be admitted that it was a strange one.

Here we are on Saturday, March 9th, back at Kisumu, our port of departure. It has been an interesting and unusual experience, this circumnavigation of the great lake, and it has been made pleasant by the society of the three white officers on board, but I think that a tourist could perhaps put in his time better by simply crossing the lake in the ordinary mail boat, seeing something of Uganda, and staying for a day or two in the Mountains of the Moon, where there is an enterprising little hotel. I am glad the voyage is over, for I am geared for work and I find nothing so exhausting as rest.

At the very last moment a shadow fell upon us, for Malcolm developed a strong attack either of sunstroke or of ptomaine poisoning, or possibly a mixture of both. I write after a long nightmare night in the train during which the poor boy has been tossing about in delirium. This morning he is conscious again and his temperature is normal, so I trust the attack will be as short as it has been severe. When once we got him to the shelter of the friendly Norfolk Hotel at Nairobi we felt that all would be well, and so it proved, for under the skilful ministration of Dr. Anderson he was soon his cheery self once more.

CHAPTER XII

The People of Nairobi – Strange Animals – A Lecture Incident
– Mombasa – The Famous Siege – An Earth-bound Animal –
Salt Water once more.

In all our wanderings we have not stayed in any place
where there are such strange varieties and sharp con-
trasts of humanity as in Nairobi. I have stood in
Government Road and made the following notes of the
passers-by. First two young English girls with short
frocks and tennis rackets who would be normal in
Norwood. Then two cotton-clad young negroes
walking, hand in hand. Then several inoffensive East
Indians in their clean white clothes and turbans. Then a
fierce-looking Mahomedan with hawk's beak and virile
beard – a Pathan from North India. Then a stout English
lady with her bag who might be shopping in Bond
Street. Then a one-garment savage with ear-rings and
trinkets. Then a pink-shirted youth in shorts, as brown
as a nut, just off safari. Then a group of Indian women
with their beautiful coloured dresses. And so in various

combinations the procession ebbs and flows. And over all is the great unseen guardian hand of the British Raj.

The bearing of the whites of Kenya to the less developed races seems to me to be all that could be desired. I have never while I have been in the country seen the least sign of intolerance or bullying. There was one case in the Courts which I record because I spoke of the South African outrages. In this instance it was an English settler who was accused of torturing a native to gain information about some suspected theft. The torture, such as it was, was a small thing compared to the usual third-degree methods of America, but it was severely commented upon by the Public Prosecutor and would probably have been duly punished were it not that the unhappy man, who was probably of deranged mind, committed suicide on the last day of the trial. It is the only case of the sort of which I have heard, and I stress the fact because I have seen allusions in the English papers as if Kenya had a bad name for its treatment of natives.

I had an interesting talk to-day with Captain Ritchie, the very capable Game Warden of Kenya, on the subject of witch doctors. Both he and his experienced assistant declared that their powers were entirely for evil and that they did undoubtedly by the force of suggestion will their victims to death. Many cases were instanced of these murders, but none of any beneficent activities save that Captain Ritchie knew one man who had four times broken up droughts and brought rain by his incantations. That the rain should follow each time after the ceremony is striking, and yet it offends all reason to think of any connection between the savage and the weather. Both the game authorities listened with attention, and, I think, with surprise, to my own experience with the Zulu witch.

In connection with Game Wardens one's thoughts go to the many strange animals some legend of which comes occasionally to the more civilized centres. Of course it is easy to deride these creatures, but we must remember that the okapi was also derided until several skins were actually brought to Europe. So we must not judge the shadowy beasts too harshly. One which has excited much attention in South Africa is a creature which can jump a 6-foot palisade with a sheep in its jaws. It is not a lion. It has committed depredations in so civilized a centre as Graaf-Reinet in Cape Province, but none know what it is. The spoor is described as "queer, round, and saucer-like, with 2-inch toenails." Another strange beast was called nsuifisi by the natives, and was said to be a striped leopard with ferocious predatory characteristics. This was ridiculed, but a well-known Rhodesian hunter actually shot one recently and it has been pronounced to be an entirely new specimen of the cheetah. This mystery has been cleared, but a more formidable one remains in the Nandi bear, or chemosit as the natives call it. Most fantastic stories are told about this creature, but the nearest approach to fact that we could reach was a reputable person in Nairobi who assured us that his cousin had been dragged off his verandah by one of them and had his scars to show. It was said to stand higher at the shoulder than a lion about 40 inches – and to be like a huge hyena. The spoor is said to show six digits, which would surely be unique among mammals. So vague are the accounts that some people assert that the creature is anthropoid and arboreal. But amid all the rumours there would seem to be some solid nucleus of fact.

There is also a creature called the lau, which is said to be an enormous snake in the immense swamps of the Soudan. It should be easy to locate by the bold hunter in that it is declared to have a prodigious bellow, especially at night. A writer in the *Bulawayo Chronicle*, to whom I owe some particulars, says that a huge water snake of an unknown kind was killed by a Greek trader in a Tanganyika lake, and that it was 40 feet long and 3 yards in girth, so that this may be a smaller relative of the Nilotic lau. There is also a huge creature which is said to live in the chasm through which the Orange River runs down to the sea. It has some saurian attributes. Only yesterday I met Count Almasy, a young Hungarian who is hunting for a four-tusked elephant, corresponding to some antedeluvian type, of the existence of which he declares himself to be assured. There is plenty of romance still to be found in the wilds of Africa. What a dull world it will be when everything has been explored, and everything explained. But there are always the infinitudes and eternities of psychic knowledge in reserve.

My last lecture at Nairobi was marked by a curious incident. Among my slides was one which represented an alleged spectre in a country house. This photograph had been sent me by a gentleman in Nottingham, who was, as I understand, one of the research party. It is not one of my more important photographs, and as I only had one witness at the back of it, I have several times declared that I could not guarantee it. On that very evening I said it was not evidential. I was, however, considerably surprised when a Mr. Palmer, a local dentist, rose and claimed that he had himself personated the ghost in order to deceive his companions. He added, however, that the real ghost had actually appeared immediately afterwards, and he stated in a letter to me next day: "After I saw and felt the power of the real ghost in that haunted Court I could not have posed again." Most people will agree that it was a pity that he posed at all, and that it is deplorable that the work of earnest and honest men should be complicated by irresponsible buffoonery. It confirms what I have often said, that it is the researcher and the spectator who have to be watched and checked quite as much as the medium. If the public could realize the number of false exposures engineered by newspaper reporters, self-advertising conjurers, young college professors who wish to seem smart, and other unscrupulous persons, they would take these charges with much reserve. There is a well-known conjurer who declared that he would think nothing of stuffing muslin into a medium's pocket in the dark, and it is notorious that the whole valuable series of Crandon experiments might have been ruined had Houdini not been detected in his manipulation to prove them fraudulent. And these are our critics! *Quis custodiet ipsos custodes?*

As to this incident in Nairobi, which is liable to be misrepresented, the following comment from an unknown friend in the *East African Standard* seems fair. He says:

> "Mr. Palmer admitted that afterwards he saw the ghost himself, which makes his interruption quite indefensible. It seems a pity that such an interesting lecture should have been interrupted in public over such an unimportant point. The photograph, as Sir Arthur explained before Mr. Palmer's voice was heard, was not evidential but interesting. It would seem that such a matter could have been discussed after the lecture rather than by a boorish attempt at a dramatic exposition of fraud which deserved the tolerant contempt with which it was received."

This is severe, but I think it is a fair statement, and I thank this stranger who signs his letter Stanley Lavers for his intervention.

It is interesting to add that, on my return to England, Mr. Melton, from whom I originally got the photograph, confirms his account, and assures me that he took it himself and that I was in no way in error.[1]

On March 13th we bade farewell to Nairobi, which will always remain with its high-spirited inhabitants a pleasant memory to all of us. If I have not converted the inhabitants to psychic truth, I have at least, as the correspondence column of the local paper would show, promoted tremendous discussion. Anything is better than apathy in religious matters. Our homeward route ran through the game preserves of the Athi Plains, and I remember saying to my wife as I settled down in a corner of the carriage, "Don't call me for anything less than a giraffe or a lion." So quickly does one become blasé.

We had three days to wait at Mombasa for our ship, and the time was not wasted as a lecture had been arranged. Meanwhile we had some pleasant drives round the island, which consists entirely of coral with a top-dressing of some feet of sandy loam. Vasco da Gama

---

[1] He has now forwarded to me the negative, so the matter is certain; and yet this fabrication, so hurtful to my work, has appeared in half the papers in England and America.

landed here in 1498, six years after Columbus discovered America. It was made the centre of the whole Portuguese coastland, its island situation offering particular facilities for defence. To this end a huge fort was built – the very nucleus of their Empire. This place was attacked by Arabs in 1696 and there followed what must surely be one of the most memorable sieges on record. For eighteen months the garrison held out, and were then strengthened by a small reinforcement which seems to have dropped from the clouds. This enabled them to hold out for yet another fifteen months. Then when wounds and disease had reduced them to eleven men and two women, they were unable to man the perimeter and the Arabs got in. All were massacred. Two days later a relief expedition arrived from Goa, but seeing that the fort was taken they sailed away.

Denis and I, under the guidance of Mr. Robertson the Governor, went over the old place, which is full of horrible memories. It is used now as a prison, which seems to be very well conducted. When the conversation turned upon the siege of 1696, I remarked that there was someone down at our hotel who probably remembered it. I could see from my host's face that this confirmed his worst suspicions. I had to explain that I was alluding to Liza, the old musty encrusted tortoise who lives in the yard and is credited with a past of 250 years. Her gnarled, elephant-like legs look very ancient indeed. She eats well, sleeps much, and makes a public nuisance of herself by blocking the traffic when she takes a walk. She is the only visible earth-bound thing we know.

The Manor Hotel at Mombasa is one which may be safely recommended to travellers. It was, I understand, designed by the two good North-country ladies who run it, and we have never seen greater ingenuity in mitigating the rigours of what is an exceedingly hot town. We quite enjoyed the few days we spent there, which were the more pleasant as we had looked forward to our stay at Mombasa with some apprehension, hearing rumours of smells and mosquitoes. As a matter of fact we have seldom been more comfortable.

But the Ocean is my nursing mother, and glad I was to be out upon its broad blue bosom once more. As I write I see the vast expanse upon my right, while to my left lies the distant East African coast up which we steam for Aden. It is the good ship *Modasa*, of the British India Line, which bears us homewards. My work is done, and I am so near it that I have not yet perhaps got the true perspective of it all. This only I know, that Spiritualism is the greatest revelation the world has ever known, and that I have proclaimed it in every town of consequence from Cape Town to Nairobi. Could I have invested six months of my small remaining stock of time more usefully than that? I think not.

CHAPTER XIII

A Lonely Ocean – Solomon's Tanks – *The Nation's Key-men*
– A Great City of the Future – A Dead Town – The Great
Pyramid – A Crowded Day – Malta – Home Again.

The sea between Mombasa and Cape Gardafui, the
eastern shoulder of Africa, is among the most lonely
which we have traversed. For a thousand miles we did
not see the sail of an Arab dhow. All the way the desert
coast of Italian Somaliland formed our western horizon,
and there also we saw no sign of life, nor was there any
upon the gentle heaving surface of the Indian Ocean. I
have wondered why the surface of the sea is not more
populous, since this is the only really fixed point save
the bottom. When the young cod has a date with his
lady one would think that the surface must be the
meeting-place, since it can hardly fix the various levels
of depth. However, as a matter of fact the surface would
seem to be the most deserted part of the ocean.

For several months in the year, notably the present
month of March, there is a constant trade wind blowing

from the North or North-East in these waters. This must have been of great use to Phœnicians, Portuguese, and all other early navigators. Then in other months, from May onwards, there comes the South-West Monsoon, which blows in the opposite direction with the force very often of a gale. With the progress of air navigation these great atmospheric currents will no doubt become of vital importance to mankind.

On March 22nd we saw "the barren rocks of Aden" looming up in front of us. The rock is an extinct volcano and is one of the Rift Valley series, a connection between those which we saw in Central Africa and the Dead Sea. I had never seen the great rainwater tanks which are attributed to King Solomon, so we went ashore to inspect them. I had no idea that they were so enormous or so well constructed. They had been choked up with rubbish for centuries, but the British have cleared them and made them workable. They seem to me to show that the country has been a very arid one for at least 3,000 years, or so elaborate a device for watering ships would not have been needed. An Arab told me that they had rain about once in three years, but that when it does come there is such a rush that the huge pits are filled up within a few hours.

Behind the town lies the great hinterland of Yemen, so little known and yet so close to the main highways of Commerce. There was a good deal of mixed fighting here during the War – the sort of fighting which meant hardship or death to many, and yet will never be understood by the world. Who knows, for example, about the 1st Battalion Yemen Light Infantry, the name of which I saw upon a Memorial?

My reading of late has been rather mixed, but it includes a book, *The Nation's Key-men*, by William Coombs, which really deserves some attention. It touches me because it is about the grievances of ships' officers, and in my wandering life I have had ample opportunities of realizing the remarkable qualities of these men, and how grave are the disabilities under which they suffer. They are in truth the most essential men in the community and the ones who are most worthy of good treatment, being responsible for so many thousands of lives and such valuable cargoes. But their pay is at the very least one-third below what it should be, while their work, as at present arranged, separates them from their families to an inhuman degree. For a captain in the Merchant Service to get three clear weeks in the year with his wife and children is quite exceptional, and for them there is no half Saturday, whole Sunday, Bank holiday, or any of the breaks which come to the ordinary civilian. This could be obviated by keeping a certain number of supernumerary officers who would occasionally relieve the usual staff. This would, of course, involve more expense, and so would

the raising of salaries. The Companies might say that
they are subjected to severe competition and that an
increase of running costs would absorb all their profits.
When, however, one looks at the enormous dividends
and bonuses distributed by the Companies during the
War – bonuses of 100 and even of 300 per cent on the
top of heavy dividends were not uncommon – one feels
that the Directors had no right to divide profits right up
to the hilt and not lay aside any assured provision on a
proper scale for the men who run the ships. One has to
remember also that the stock of many of the great
Companies has been heavily watered, so that the figures
now do not represent the true position, and a modest
dividend of 7 or 8 per cent may really represent far
more than this on the original capital. It is a question
which should be examined by a strong Commission, and
the cause of these officers should be taken up by some
Parliamentarian who would be as wholehearted as
Plimsoll was in his day. So long as firms managed their
own business and were comparatively small, there were
human relations between employers and employed; but
in these days of large combines, when the whole interests of the shipowners are put into the hands of the
Shipowners' Federation, the officers are helpless. It is,
however, a serious state of things that these men, who
are so necessary to the nation, should be deeply discon-
tented. One of the first recommendations of a

Commission would, I think, be that a check should be put upon the numbers of new candidates for a profession which is already overmanned. These remarks, I may add, are not founded upon one book or upon a few men, but upon a fairly wide acquaintance with the needs of our Mercantile Marine.

All this is digression, however, and I must get back to the Red Sea, up which we are now steadily booming. I have no notion why it was ever called "Red", for looking out of the port-hole as I write it seems to me to be the very bluest bit of water that I have seen. The boys and I spend part of our time, together with that admirable baritone Eric Marshall, in leaning over the prow, and looking straight down the line of the forefoot into the depths. In this way we have seen several strange fish before they have been disturbed by the rush of the vessel. Several sharks, many dolphins, a turtle, a green sea snake, a pipe fish and others were on our list. To-day, March 23rd, we are past the Twelve Apostle rocks and we expect to-morrow to halt at Port Soudan.

This place was a great surprise to me. There is no doubt in my mind that it is destined to be a considerable city, though it was only founded in our own time. When the idea first took root of sending a short-cut railway from the Red Sea to tap the Soudan, the old port of Suakim was made the terminus. Presently, however, it became apparent that navigation there was very difficult, and that another bay some 40 miles to the north was very much more convenient. Therefore this town was established, and as it is the only direct outlet, and as the output of the Soudan continually increases, it will soon be a city. Already the harbour is crowded with shipping; it is fitted up with modern loading and unloading tackle, and it has huge warehouses and all the other appurtenances of a well-run port. We found 2,000 tons of cargo – mostly cotton seeds to be converted into oil – waiting for us, and the quays were piled with other cargoes. It is a great centre of industry.

The disadvantage – or the advantage – according to how it suits one, in travelling by ships which are mainly cargo vessels is that you can never tell where you may be hung up and all your dates become uncertain. We shall not touch Marseilles with the majestic right-to-the-tick precision with which the great Cape liners come booming round Robin's Island. In this particular case it was clear that at least a day would pass before our stuff was aboard, and a ship is no pleasant residence when three winches are clattering and thumping all day. The boys and Billy were content to have a swim in the coral-enclosed bathing-place, and afterwards to fish for sharks; but my wife and I thought that we would go by train to Suakim and see that quaint old town which was only 42 miles away. The line runs across a parched desert all the way with camel scrub and low mimosa bushes here and there. We passed the field of Handoub, where the Egyptian column was massacred, and we must have been near El Teb, where the British avenged their death. The train drew up some distance from the town, and we had a very tiring walk in the heat of the day before we got back to the welcome shade of our carriage. One passes through the so-called Gordon Gate which pierces the old brown wall of coral rock which surrounds the city. Inside we came upon an outer town which was fairly populous, and then crossing a bridge, we entered the old city, which covers the end of the peninsula and has the sea all round it. It is a nightmare place – a city of the dead. It is composed of huge ancient white houses with much decorative woodwork, the houses once of rich merchants or noblemen, but the whole place is as dead as Pompeii. We saw no single living soul in all the streets save two Arabs upon the quay who were gutting a great pile of silvery fish which looked like bream. It was like some impossible place seen in a dream. The wonderful blue water, turning to emerald green in the shallows, and broken by gleaming golden sandbanks, lapped right up to the huge white tomb-like houses. Finally we made our way back to the waiting train.

Tourists should bear in mind that any representation of the human body is distasteful to Moslems and that photography is unpopular among them. This is of less importance when you are in populous centres, but on the outskirts of civilization it may lead to awkward situations. As we returned there were two fierce-looking, mahogany-faced Arabs standing talking at the Gordon Gate. My wife and I halted to look at them, for they were the real desert breed with swords at their sides. When my wife made a motion with her camera, one of them with a scowl drew his tunic aside and grasped the hilt of the dagger in his sash. My wife with great tact swept her hand round to show that it was the old gate which she intended to take. The man still looked sulky, but the incident was closed. On the same day a Fuzzy attacked Eric Marshall, the singer, for the same reason on the quay beside the ship. There are no troops apparently in this region, and few police, so that the very virile war-like natives have it rather their own way.

This ship is full of officials and planters going home for a rest – a fine set of people with many bonny children who seem to refute the theory of racial degeneration in the tropics. One gets good information by talking to such folk – the real pioneers of Empire. I was surprised at some of the facts regarding Tanganyika, lately German East Africa, which were given me by one who was well up in the subject. Already the exports of this Colony are ahead of those of Kenya, which is explained by the fact that though Kenya has at least 12,000 whites as against 5,000 in Tanganyika, there are

4,500,000 natives in Tanganyika, against about half that number in Kenya. These natives have taken to coffee planting and other industries on their own, and it is they who have swollen the exports, which work out roughly at £3,800,000 for Tanganyika and £3,300,600 for Kenya. The theories of the two States are, as I have tried to show, quite opposed to each other. Kenya wishes to be a white man's country. Tanganyika tries to be a black man's country with white superintendence. The contest between these two ideals is a matter of vast importance to the Empire.

This experienced planter, a most reasonable man, assured me that all the conclusions which I have given as to the uselessness of the Missions from a religious point of view were absolutely sound. The White Fathers (Catholic) were the best, also the German Lutheran, but the Mahomedan were more fitted to the native needs and mentality. On the other hand as civilizing centres and for medical instruction the Missions were valuable. Their religious teaching merely puzzled the natives, who could not understand the rival doctrines of so many sects.

On Friday, March 29th, we accomplished what I really think must be a record for one day's hustle. No one could fit more vivid impressions into a single date, and though much of it was familiar to me it was all new to the youngsters and we got their reflected pleasure. We left the ship at Suez at six in the morning and motored for a hundred miles over as forbidding a desert as is to be found in the world, until we descended upon Cairo. It is amazing how this city has progressed. Everywhere as we traversed it I saw signs of growth and opulence which make it the worthy capital of a nation. I knew the place well in 1896, and yet there is much of it which I could not have recognized, so great are the improvements.

After a halt at Shepheard's Hotel we pushed on to the Pyramids and the Sphinx. From Mena the rest of the family mounted upon camels and went up to see the sights, while I waited for them on the verandah of the Mena Hotel. For an hour or more I contemplated the opening of the Great Pyramid, examining with my glasses the perfect masonry of the stones which form the angle above the door. These huge monoliths meet with the most absolute accuracy. I am not a British Israelite, for I do not believe that in 3,000 years a race could change its characteristics, but on the other hand I do not envy the man who can without awe and wonder contemplate the tremendous problem which the Pyramid presents. It is not possible to doubt that the direction and the height of the passages have a definite meaning, and what that meaning may be, and why it was plugged off by a granite block so that no human eye should see it, is the greatest riddle which one generation has ever left for another. There is a message there, and the one valid argument that the message is meant for the British people is that we are the only ones who have preserved the inch as a measure and that it would seem that the inch is the unit of any stone cipher which may lie in this building. This might conceivably be true, however, without identifying us with Semitic ancestors. It must be admitted that it is a very extraordinary coincidence, if it is indeed a coincidence, that the measurements should coincide so much as they have been shown to do, with definite dates in history. But here again there is no need to call in any direct Divine interposition. We had many seers, and if their prophecies had been embodied in stone they might well seem wonderful, yet they would only be using a not very uncommon psychic faculty which may have been clearer and fuller in ancient days than now.

So I mused as I sat watching the wonderful structure until the camel-riders returned – Malcolm much dishevelled and lamenting the absence of a steering wheel. Back we went 7 miles to Cairo, lunched, and got away to the Museum to see the King Tut relics, which are certainly most marvellous. A rather weak and kindly face the young man had – he was only twenty-eight when he died. How strange that after nearly forty centuries we know more about his *ménage* than that of any monarch in history. It was certainly sumptuous. I cannot suppose that for artistic design and colouring, and the skilful fitting of precious stones and metals, we could equal the wonders that we saw – case after case until they seemed endless. Some had only arrived the week before for the grave still gives up its secrets. If these were the trappings of royalty, and if the nobles dressed to correspond, then the old Court of Egypt must have been a wonder scene of magnificence.

From the Museum we passed to the Mosque of Mahomet Ali, a great soldier and a bloody-minded scoundrel who murdered the whole of his own body-guard and who cut off the hands of the architect of the Mosque that it might be his final work. It is smaller and less ornate than St. Sophia, but it is more delicately fashioned and out of more precious material. Thence we passed out to the Citadel, where in a corner a crowd of British Tommies, men of the South Wales Borderers, were seated. The infantry do not seem to be numerous in the city, and being mostly very young soldiers they do not compare favourably in physique with the older Egyptians, but they are smart, clear-eyed, bright-looking lads and would give a good account of themselves. The airmen are numerous in their dark blue uniforms, and I noticed some gunners and men of the Tank Corps. I was surprised to see that as a consequence of street assaults, against which a bayonet is a poor weapon, every soldier carried a life-preserver, a wooden handle with a metal head slung to his belt. It was one of several proofs that under a calm surface there were unseen currents.

From the Citadel we went to the Bazaar, and thence, after much shopping, to Shepheard's Hotel once more, and thence to catch the six o'clock train to Port Said, which we reached about ten o'clock, rejoining our ship, which had just made the transit of the Canal. I think that there have been few days in our lives more full of impressions than that.

Here we are out in the Mediterranean and approaching Malta, which we should reach to-night. The air is cold with a virile north wind in our faces, but the sunlit sea stretches in a deep blue circle around us unbroken by a shadow or a sail. It reminds me of the audacious simile of dear old Frank Bullen – I am not sure if it is blasphemous or magnificent – when he compares such a sea with the pupil of God's eye.

I gave a lecture on Spiritualism on Saturday and had an excellent and attentive audience, including, I am glad to say, many of the ship's company. I always take as conservative a view as is possible of present religious conditions, pointing out that it is one thing to scrape the barnacles off the bottom the old ship which has carried us so long, and quite another thing to scrape a hole in the bottom and scuttle her completely. But the futility and unreality of our observances must have been impressed upon them next day at the Easter Sunday service, where the first lesson enjoined us that for ever and ever, under pain of the wrath of God, we were at that time to kill a goat or sheep, to eat it with bitter herbs and to burn the remainder. That was the Christian message for Easter Sunday! It is dusty, musty, out-of-date stuff of this sort, bearing no sort of relation to our lives, which disgusts people with religion as it is presented to them, and makes them reject it all, instead of discriminating between the Divine essence and the human absurdities.

I have spent the day – a part of it – in drawing up a letter for our psychic papers containing my views as to our action in the coming General Election. It is of course an individual effort, since I hold no official position, unless indeed the presidentship of the international federation and of the London Spiritualist Alliance gives me one. The folly of the Home Office under Sir William Joynson Hicks in persecuting not only our mediums but even the officials of our Societies has made it impossible, as it seems to me, to support his party. Of the two other parties we should, I think, support the one which gives us fullest assurances. We have no desire to uphold cheats or charlatans, but at present the very existence of spiritual powers is in practice denied by the law of England, and the Apostolic circle would have been as liable to criminal arrest as are our mediums. This is an intolerable situation, and I think that if we show our political power we shall set it right. We are not a feeble folk. At the recent plebiscite of the *Daily News* 7,500 voted that we were in the right, and less than 3,000 that we were wrong.

We had only a few hours at Malta, but we were amazed at the fine buildings and general prosperity and picturesqueness of Valetta. I was particularly interested in the relics of the Knights of St. John, since I have the honour to be a Knight of St. John myself. I wish we all looked like the fine statue of the Grand Master of the Order, who stands with his hands on the hilt of his sword, midway down the main street, still wearing that stern frown with which he confronted Barbarossa and his men. The great walls and moats still exist which he defended so well. These Hospitallers outlasted the Order of the Temple by centuries, showing the higher estimation in which they were held.

As we left Malta we passed the mouth of the bay which is the legendary scene of Paul's shipwreck and which is still called after him. I have little doubt that it is the real place, for Paul was already a well-known man – so well known that the Christians of Rome came out nearly a day's journey to meet him on his arrival. Therefore the details of his great adventure would certainly be eagerly discussed, and it would not be likely that any serious mistake would be made as to its scene. We Spiritualists may well honour Paul, for he was the first who ever made a list of the gifts of a medium.

It is a long jump from Paul to modern machinery, but on the same day I went down into our engine room to examine the oil-driven turbines. The opinion of marine engineers seems to be that, in spite of the temporary advantages of oil, which greatly diminish the number of stokers, coal will still prevail. The latest development is an invention for reducing coal to a fine powder, and then blowing it, as the oil is blown, through tubes into the furnace. Several ships are already fitted thus, and the device seems to have a future.

This has been the most uneventful voyage which I have ever experienced. In all these thousands of miles we have hardly been conscious of the movement of the vessel. I think of my Zulu seer with her prophecy that we should all go safely and happily across the dark waters with my mission well done. In a ship much depends upon the captain, and where all are such good fellows it is invidious to single one out for praise. But this I can truly say of Captain Gilchrist, that he takes more care of his ship and its contents than any captain with whom I have sailed. Not only have we several times been compelled, sometimes at awkward moments, to don our lifebelts and to muster upon deck, but twice a week the boats are swung outboard to show that all the tackle is in good order. I am sure that in many a ship if this were tried it would be found that the falls would not run through the sheaves, or the davits were rusted, or something was amiss. I know of what I speak, for I have seen it tried. I think that the Board of Trade would do well to make it compulsory that within a week of the start of a long voyage there should be a drill and a trial of the boats.

And now the end has come. On our port bow lies the rocky headland of Sardinia. Upon the starboard are the snow-clad peaks of Corsica. We are in the Straits of Bonefacio. In front of us lies the Gulf of Lions (not of Lyons, as many are surprised to learn), and our bowsprit points to Marseilles. Within a day our long journey will be done.

And I close this record of it with a grateful heart. I turn to the first lines of it, and I see again the New Forest lawn with the brown leaves sweeping across it, and the great trees bending to the October gale. I know now that I will find it in the fresh verdure of Spring. Between the fall of those leaves and their rebirth how much has happened to me and to mine! But we set forth with a purpose, and that purpose has been fulfilled even more than our fondest hopes could have supposed. We come back, each of us, stronger in health, more earnest in our beliefs, more eager to fight once more in the greatest of all causes, the cause of the regeneration of religion and of the restoration of that direct and practical spiritual element which is the one and only antidote to scientific Materialism. For this and manifold mercies we do, each and all, most humbly return our thanks to those unseen ones who have ever been our helpers and companions.

APPENDIX

The following may be of interest to those who are open to the idea of other-world telepathic communication. It came as recorded in the text as we sat in respectful silence by the grave of Cecil Rhodes. We had been warned by a Cape Town medium that we would receive a message. It was written down by my wife's hand. Our interpolations are in brackets. When the hand became agitated we asked:

(Do you believe in God?)
God bless you. I do.
(Can this be Cecil Rhodes who writes?)
This way I came and I went to my destiny, partly of happiness and partly of regret. But here one makes up for missed opportunities.
(Is it really you, Mr. Rhodes?)
Yes, it is I.
(It is indeed a privilege to speak with you. Your work on earth was wonderful.)
No, sir. It can never be as wonderful as religious work –

not by many leagues. Religious work is world work. My energies affected only a small area.

(Was the message true from Groote Schuur?)

I was there. I have been wanting to get in touch with you for I value the effect such teaching will have upon the world's ultimate destiny. Your own burial place will be in the souls and hearts of men. We shall meet anon and what talks we shall have.

(I shall be honoured.)

We will visit the old new earth together.

(Is Dr. Jameson with you?)

We work together over here. We want to purify this glorious country from the dross and mirk and growth of human fungus which have arisen from the bowels of the earth.

(We wish we had brought up some flowers.)

The thought has created flowers.

(We go now. God bless you, Mr. Rhodes.)

And may His angels keep and guard and uphold you, until the great crossing into the world of light – a light so great that the human mind cannot conceive the fulfilment of all that the soul unconsciously craves for. Here is its realization.